Ballades & Rhymes in Blue China and Rhymes a la Mode

Andrew Lang

Alpha Editions

This edition published in 2024

ISBN : 9789366383798

Design and Setting By
Alpha Editions
www.alphaedis.com
Email - info@alphaedis.com

As per information held with us this book is in Public Domain.
This book is a reproduction of an important historical work. Alpha Editions uses the best technology to reproduce historical work in the same manner it was first published to preserve its original nature. Any marks or number seen are left intentionally to preserve its true form.

INTRODUCTION

THIRTY years have passed, like a watch in the night, since the earlier of the two sets of verses here reprinted, *Ballades in Blue China*, was published. At first there were but twenty-two *Ballades*; ten more were added later. They appeared in a little white vellum wrapper, with a little blue Chinese singer copied from a porcelain jar; and the frontispiece was a little design by an etcher now famous.

Thirty years ago blue china was a kind of fetish in some circles, æsthetic circles, of which the balladist was not a member.

The *ballade* was an old French form of verse, in France revived by Théodore de Banville, and restored to an England which had long forgotten the Middle Ages, by my friends Mr. Austin Dobson and Mr. Edmund Gosse. They, so far as I can trust my memory, were the first to reintroduce these pleasant old French *nugae*, while an anonymous author let loose upon the town a whole winged flock of *ballades* of amazing dexterity. This unknown balladist was Mr. Henley; perhaps he was the first Englishman who ever burst into a *double ballade*, and his translations of two of Villon's ballades into modern thieves' slang were marvels of dexterity. Mr. Swinburne wrote a serious *ballade*, but the form, I venture to think, is not 'wholly serious,' of its nature, in modern days; and he did not persevere. Nor did the taste for these trifles long endure. A good *ballade* is almost as rare as a good sonnet, but a middling *ballade* is almost as easily written as the majority of sonnets. Either form readily becomes mechanical, cheap and facile. I have heard Mr. George Meredith improvise a sonnet, a Petrarchian sonnet, obedient to the rules, without pen and paper. He spoke 'and the numbers came'; he sonneted as easily as a living poet, in his Eton days, improvised Latin elegiacs and Greek hexameters.

The sonnet endures. Mr. Horace Hutchinson wrote somewhere: "When you have read a sonnet, you feel that though there does not seem to be much of it, you have done a good deal, as when you have eaten a cold hard-boiled egg." Still people keep on writing sonnets, because the sonnet is wholly serious. In an English sonnet you cannot easily be flippant of pen. A few great poets have written immortal sonnets—among them are Milton, Wordsworth, and Keats. Thus the sonnet is a thing which every poet thinks it worth while to try at; like Felix Arvers, he may be made immortal by a single sonnet. Even I have written one too many! Every anthologist wants to anthologise it (*The Odyssey*); it never was a favourite of my own, though it had the honour to be kindly spoken of by Mr. Matthew Arnold.

On the other hand, no man since François Villon has been immortalised by a single ballade—*Mais où sont les neiges d'antan?*

To speak in any detail about these poor ballades would be to indite a part of an autobiography. Looking back at the little book, 'what memories it stirs' in one to whom

> 'Fate has done this wrong,
> That I should write too much and live too long.'

The Ballade of the Tweed, and the *Rhymes à la Mode*, were dedicated to the dearest of kinsmen, a cricketer and angler. The *Ballade of Roulette* was inscribed to R. R., a gallant veteran of the Indian Mutiny, a leader of Light Horse, whose father was a friend of Sir Walter Scott. He was himself a Borderer, in whose defeats on the green field of Roulette I often shared, long, long ago.

So many have gone 'into the world of light' that it is a happiness to think of him to whom *The Ballade of Golf* was dedicated, and to remember that he is still capable of scoring his double century at cricket, and of lifting the ball high over the trees beyond the boundaries of a great cricket-field. Perhaps Mr. Leslie Balfour-Melville will pardon me for mentioning his name, linked as it is with so many common memories. 'One is taken and another left.'

A different sort of memory attaches itself to *A Ballade of Dead Cities*. It was written in a Theocritean amoebean way, in competition with Mr. Edmund Gosse; he need not be ashamed of the circumstance, for another shepherd, who was umpire, awarded the prize (two kids just severed from their dams) to his victorious muse.

The *Ballade of the Midnight Forest*, the Ballade of the Huntress Artemis, was translated from Théodore de Banville, whose beautiful poem came so near the Greek, that when the late Provost of Oriel translated a part of its English shadow into Greek hexameters, you might suppose, as you read, that they were part of a lost Homeric Hymn.

I never wrote a *double ballade*, and stanzas four and five of the *Double Ballade of Primitive Man* were contributed by the learned *doyen* of Anthropology, Mr. E. B. Tylor, author of Primitive Culture.

À tout seigneur tout honneur!

In *Ballade of his Choice of a Sepulchre*, the Windburg is a hill in Teviotdale. *A Portrait of 1783* was written on a French engraving after Morland, and *Benedetta Ramus* was addressed to a mezzotint (an artist's proof, 'very rare'). It is after Romney and is 'My Beauty,' as Charles Lamb said (once, unluckily, to a Scot) of an engraving, after Lionardo, of some fair dead lady.

The sonnet, *Natural Theology*, is the germ of what the author has since written, in *The Making of Religion*, on the long neglected fact that many of the lowest savages known share the belief in a benevolent All Father and Judge of men.

Concerning verses in *Rhymes à la Mode*, visitors to St. Andrews may be warned not to visit St. Leonard's Chapel, described in the second stanza of *Almae Matres*. In the writer's youth, and even in middle age,

> He loitered idly where the tall
>   Fresh-budded mountain-ashes blow
> Within its desecrated wall.

The once beautiful ruins carpeted with grass and wild flowers have been doubly desecrated by persons, academic persons, having authority and a plentiful lack of taste. The slim mountain-ashes, fair as the young palm-tree that Odysseus saw beside the shrine of Apollo in Delos, have been cut down by the academic persons to whom power is given. The grass and flowers have been rooted up. Hideous little wooden fences enclose the grave slabs: a roof of a massive kind has been dumped down on the old walls, and the windows, once so graceful in their airy lines, have been glazed in a horrible manner, while the ugly iron gate precludes entrance to a shrine which is now a black and dismal dungeon.

> "Oh, be that roof as lead to lead
> Above the dull Restorer's head,
> A Minstrel's malison is said!"

Notes explanatory are added to the Rhymes, and their information, however valuable, need not here be repeated.

BALLADES IN BLUE CHINA

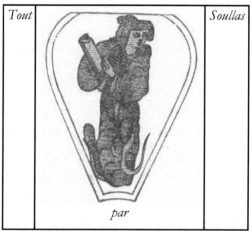

A BALLADE OF XXXII BALLADES.

Friend, when you bear a care-dulled eye,
And brow perplexed with things of weight,
And fain would bid some charm untie
The bonds that hold you all too strait,
Behold a solace to your fate,
Wrapped in this cover's china blue;
These ballades fresh and delicate,
This dainty troop of Thirty-two!

The mind, unwearied, longs to fly
And commune with the wise and great;
But that same ether, rare and high,
Which glorifies its worthy mate,
To breath forspent is disparate:
Laughing and light and airy-new
These come to tickle the dull pate,
This dainty troop of Thirty-two.

Most welcome then, when you and I,
Forestalling days for mirth too late,
To quips and cranks and fantasy
Some choice half-hour dedicate,
They weave their dance with measured rate
Of rhymes enlinked in order due,

Till frowns relax and cares abate,
This dainty troop of Thirty-two.

ENVOY.

Princes, of toys that please your state
Quainter are surely none to view
Than these which pass with tripping gait,
This dainty troop of Thirty-two.

F. P.

TO
AUSTIN DOBSON.

Un Livre est un ami qui change—quelquefois.
1880.
1888

BALLADE TO THEOCRITUS, IN WINTER.

ἐσορῶν τὰν Σικελὰν ἐς ἅλα.

Id. viii. 56.

Ah! leave the smoke, the wealth, the roar
Of London, and the bustling street,
For still, by the Sicilian shore,
The murmur of the Muse is sweet.
Still, still, the suns of summer greet
The mountain-grave of Helikê,
And shepherds still their songs repeat
Where breaks the blue Sicilian sea.

What though they worship Pan no more,
That guarded once the shepherd's seat,
They chatter of their rustic lore,
They watch the wind among the wheat:
Cicalas chirp, the young lambs bleat,
Where whispers pine to cypress tree;
They count the waves that idly beat
Where breaks the blue Sicilian sea.

Theocritus! thou canst restore
The pleasant years, and over-fleet;
With thee we live as men of yore,
We rest where running waters meet:
And then we turn unwilling feet
And seek the world—so must it be—

We may not linger in the heat
Where breaks the blue Sicilian sea!

ENVOY.

    Master,—when rain, and snow, and sleet
    And northern winds are wild, to thee
    We come, we rest in thy retreat,
    Where breaks the blue Sicilian sea!

BALLADE OF CLEOPATRA'S NEEDLE.

    Ye giant shades of RA and TUM,
    Ye ghosts of gods Egyptian,
    If murmurs of our planet come
    To exiles in the precincts wan
    Where, fetish or Olympian,
    To help or harm no more ye list,
    Look down, if look ye may, and scan
    This monument in London mist!

    Behold, the hieroglyphs are dumb
    That once were read of him that ran
    When seistron, cymbal, trump, and drum
    Wild music of the Bull began;
    When through the chanting priestly clan
    Walk'd Ramses, and the high sun kiss'd
    This stone, with blessing scored and ban—
    This monument in London mist.

    The stone endures though gods be numb;
    Though human effort, plot, and plan
    Be sifted, drifted, like the sum
    Of sands in wastes Arabian.
    What king may deem him more than man,
    What priest says Faith can Time resist
    While *this* endures to mark their span—
    This monument in London mist?

ENVOY.

    Prince, the stone's shade on your divan
    Falls; it is longer than ye wist:
    It preaches, as Time's gnomon can,
    This monument in London mist!

BALLADE OF ROULETTE.

TO R. R.

This life—one was thinking to-day,
In the midst of a medley of fancies—
Is a game, and the board where we play
Green earth with her poppies and pansies.
Let *manque* be faded romances,
Be *passe* remorse and regret;
Hearts dance with the wheel as it dances—
The wheel of Dame Fortune's roulette.

The lover will stake as he may
His heart on his Peggies and Nancies;
The girl has her beauty to lay;
The saint has his prayers and his trances;
The poet bets endless expanses
In Dreamland; the scamp has his debt:
How they gaze at the wheel as it glances—
The wheel of Dame Fortune's roulette!

The Kaiser will stake his array
Of sabres, of Krupps, and of lances;
An Englishman punts with his pay,
And glory the *jeton* of France is;
Your artists, or Whistlers or Vances,
Have voices or colours to bet;
Will you moan that its motion askance is—
The wheel of Dame Fortune's roulette?

ENVOY.

The prize that the pleasure enhances?
The prize is—at last to forget
The changes, the chops, and the chances—
The wheel of Dame Fortune's roulette.

BALLADE OF SLEEP.

The hours are passing slow,
I hear their weary tread
Clang from the tower, and go
Back to their kinsfolk dead.
Sleep! death's twin brother dread!
Why dost thou scorn me so?
The wind's voice overhead
Long wakeful here I know,
And music from the steep

    Where waters fall and flow.
    Wilt thou not hear me, Sleep?

    All sounds that might bestow
    Rest on the fever'd bed,
    All slumb'rous sounds and low
    Are mingled here and wed,
    And bring no drowsihed.
    Shy dreams flit to and fro
    With shadowy hair dispread;
    With wistful eyes that glow,
    And silent robes that sweep.
    Thou wilt not hear me; no?
    Wilt thou not hear me, Sleep?

    What cause hast thou to show
    Of sacrifice unsped?
    Of all thy slaves below
    I most have labourèd
    With service sung and said;
    Have cull'd such buds as blow,
    Soft poppies white and red,
    Where thy still gardens grow,
    And Lethe's waters weep.
    Why, then, art thou my foe?
    Wilt thou not hear me, Sleep?

ENVOY.

    Prince, ere the dark be shred
    By golden shafts, ere low
    And long the shadows creep:
    Lord of the wand of lead,
    Soft-footed as the snow,
    Wilt thou not hear me, Sleep!

BALLADE OF THE MIDNIGHT FOREST.

AFTER THÉODORE DE BANVILLE.

    Still sing the mocking fairies, as of old,
    Beneath the shade of thorn and holly-tree;
    The west wind breathes upon them, pure and cold,
    And wolves still dread Diana roaming free
    In secret woodland with her company.
    'Tis thought the peasants' hovels know her rite
    When now the wolds are bathed in silver light,

And first the moonrise breaks the dusky grey,
Then down the dells, with blown soft hair and bright,
And through the dim wood Dian threads her way.

With water-weeds twined in their locks of gold
The strange cold forest-fairies dance in glee,
Sylphs over-timorous and over-bold
Haunt the dark hollows where the dwarf may be,
The wild red dwarf, the nixies' enemy;
Then 'mid their mirth, and laughter, and affright,
The sudden Goddess enters, tall and white,
With one long sigh for summers pass'd away;
The swift feet tear the ivy nets outright
And through the dim wood Dian threads her way.

She gleans her silvan trophies; down the wold
She hears the sobbing of the stags that flee
Mixed with the music of the hunting roll'd,
But her delight is all in archery,
And naught of ruth and pity wotteth she
More than her hounds that follow on the flight;
The goddess draws a golden bow of might
And thick she rains the gentle shafts that slay.
She tosses loose her locks upon the night,
And through the dim wood Dian threads her way.

ENVOY.

Prince, let us leave the din, the dust, the spite,
The gloom and glare of towns, the plague, the blight:
Amid the forest leaves and fountain spray
There is the mystic home of our delight,
And through the dim wood Dian threads her way.

BALLADE OF THE TWEED.

(LOWLAND SCOTCH.)

TO T. W. LANG.

The ferox rins in rough Loch Awe,
A weary cry frae ony toun;
The Spey, that loups o'er linn and fa',
They praise a' ither streams aboon;
They boast their braes o' bonny Doon:
Gie *me* to hear the ringing reel,

Where shilfas sing, and cushats croon
By fair Tweed-side, at Ashiesteel!

There's Ettrick, Meggat, Ail, and a',
Where trout swim thick in May and June;
Ye'll see them take in showers o' snaw
Some blinking, cauldrife April noon:
Rax ower the palmer and march-broun,
And syne we'll show a bonny creel,
In spring or simmer, late or soon,
By fair Tweed-side, at Ashiesteel!

There's mony a water, great or sma',
Gaes singing in his siller tune,
Through glen and heugh, and hope and shaw,
Beneath the sun-licht or the moon:
But set us in our fishing-shoon
Between the Caddon-burn and Peel,
And syne we'll cross the heather broun
By fair Tweed-side at Ashiesteel!

ENVOY.

Deil take the dirty, trading loon
Wad gar the water ca' his wheel,
And drift his dyes and poisons doun
By fair Tweed-side at Ashiesteel!

BALLADE OF THE BOOK-HUNTER.

In torrid heats of late July,
In March, beneath the bitter *bise*,
He book-hunts while the loungers fly,—
He book-hunts, though December freeze;
In breeches baggy at the knees,
And heedless of the public jeers,
For these, for these, he hoards his fees,—
Aldines, Bodonis, Elzevirs.

No dismal stall escapes his eye,
He turns o'er tomes of low degrees,
There soiled romanticists may lie,
Or Restoration comedies;
Each tract that flutters in the breeze
For him is charged with hopes and fears,
In mouldy novels fancy sees
Aldines, Bodonis, Elzevirs.

With restless eyes that peer and spy,
Sad eyes that heed not skies nor trees,
In dismal nooks he loves to pry,
Whose motto evermore is *Spes*!
But ah! the fabled treasure flees;
Grown rarer with the fleeting years,
In rich men's shelves they take their ease,—
Aldines, Bodonis, Elzevirs!

ENVOY.

Prince, all the things that tease and please,—
Fame, hope, wealth, kisses, cheers, and tears,
What are they but such toys as these—
Aldines, Bodonis, Elzevirs?

BALLADE OF THE VOYAGE TO CYTHERA.

AFTER THÉODORE DE BANVILLE.

I know Cythera long is desolate;
I know the winds have stripp'd the gardens green.
Alas, my friends! beneath the fierce sun's weight
A barren reef lies where Love's flowers have been,
Nor ever lover on that coast is seen!
So be it, but we seek a fabled shore,
To lull our vague desires with mystic lore,
To wander where Love's labyrinths beguile;
There let us land, there dream for evermore:
"It may be we shall touch the happy isle."

The sea may be our sepulchre. If Fate,
If tempests wreak their wrath on us, serene
We watch the bolt of heaven, and scorn the hate
Of angry gods that smite us in their spleen.
Perchance the jealous mists are but the screen
That veils the fairy coast we would explore.
Come, though the sea be vex'd, and breakers roar,
Come, for the air of this old world is vile,
Haste we, and toil, and faint not at the oar;
"It may be we shall touch the happy isle."

Grey serpents trail in temples desecrate
Where Cypris smiled, the golden maid, the queen,
And ruined is the palace of our state;
But happy Loves flit round the mast, and keen
The shrill wind sings the silken cords between.

Heroes are we, with wearied hearts and sore,
Whose flower is faded and whose locks are hoar,
Yet haste, light skiffs, where myrtle thickets smile;
Love's panthers sleep 'mid roses, as of yore:
"It may be we shall touch the happy isle!"

ENVOY.

Sad eyes! the blue sea laughs, as heretofore.
Ah, singing birds your happy music pour!
Ah, poets, leave the sordid earth awhile;
Flit to these ancient gods we still adore:
"It may be we shall touch the happy isle!"

BALLADE OF THE SUMMER TERM.

(Being a Petition, in the form of a Ballade, praying the University Commissioners to spare the Summer Term.)

When Lent and Responsions are ended,
When May with fritillaries waits,
When the flower of the chestnut is splendid,
When drags are at all of the gates
(Those drags the philosopher "slates"
With a scorn that is truly sublime), [35]
Life wins from the grasp of the Fates
Sweet hours and the fleetest of time!

When wickets are bowl'd and defended,
When Isis is glad with "the Eights,"
When music and sunset are blended,
When Youth and the summer are mates,
When Freshmen are heedless of "Greats,"
And when note-books are cover'd with rhyme,
Ah, these are the hours that one rates—
Sweet hours and the fleetest of time!

When the brow of the Dean is unbended
At luncheons and mild tête-à-têtes,
When the Tutor's in love, nor offended
By blunders in tenses or dates;
When bouquets are purchased of Bates,
When the bells in their melody chime,
When unheeded the Lecturer prates—
Sweet hours and the fleetest of time!

ENVOY.

Reformers of Schools and of States,
Is mirth so tremendous a crime?
Ah! spare what grim pedantry hates—
Sweet hours and the fleetest of time!

BALLADE OF THE MUSE.

Quem tu, Melpomene, semel.

The man whom once, Melpomene,
Thou look'st on with benignant sight,
Shall never at the Isthmus be
A boxer eminent in fight,
Nor fares he foremost in the flight
Of Grecian cars to victory,
Nor goes with Delian laurels dight,
The man thou lov'st, Melpomene!

Not him the Capitol shall see,
As who hath crush'd the threats and might
Of monarchs, march triumphantly;
But Fame shall crown him, in his right
Of all the Roman lyre that smite
The first; so woods of Tivoli
Proclaim him, so her waters bright,
The man thou lov'st, Melpomene!

The sons of queenly Rome count *me*,
Me too, with them whose chants delight,—
The poets' kindly company;
Now broken is the tooth of spite,
But thou, that temperest aright
The golden lyre, all, all to thee
He owes—life, fame, and fortune's height—
The man thou lov'st, Melpomene!

ENVOY.

Queen, that to mute lips could'st unite
The wild swan's dying melody!
Thy gifts, ah! how shall he requite—
The man thou lov'st, Melpomene?

BALLADE AGAINST THE JESUITS.

AFTER LA FONTAINE.

Rome does right well to censure all the vain
Talk of Jansenius, and of them who preach
That earthly joys are damnable! 'Tis plain
We need not charge at Heaven as at a breach;
No, amble on! We'll gain it, one and all;
The narrow path's a dream fantastical,
And Arnauld's quite superfluously driven
Mirth from the world. We'll scale the heavenly wall,
Escobar makes a primrose path to heaven!

He does not hold a man may well be slain
Who vexes with unseasonable speech,
You *may* do murder for five ducats gain,
Not for a pin, a ribbon, or a peach;
He ventures (most consistently) to teach
That there are certain cases that befall
When perjury need no good man appal,
And life of love (he says) may keep a leaven.
Sure, hearing this, a grateful world will bawl,
"Escobar makes a primrose path to heaven!"

"For God's sake read me somewhat in the strain
Of his most cheering volumes, I beseech!"
Why should I name them all? a mighty train—
So many, none may know the name of each.
Make these your compass to the heavenly beach,
These only in your library instal:
Burn Pascal and his fellows, great and small,
Dolts that in vain with Escobar have striven;
I tell you, and the common voice doth call,
Escobar makes a primrose path to heaven!

ENVOY.

Satan, that pride did hurry to thy fall,
Thou porter of the grim infernal hall—
Thou keeper of the courts of souls unshriven!
To shun thy shafts, to 'scape thy hellish thrall,
Escobar makes a primrose path to heaven!

BALLADE OF DEAD CITIES.

TO E. W. GOSSE.

The dust of Carthage and the dust
Of Babel on the desert wold,
The loves of Corinth, and the lust,

Orchomenos increased with gold;
The town of Jason, over-bold,
And Cherson, smitten in her prime—
What are they but a dream half-told?
Where are the cities of old time?

In towns that were a kingdom's trust,
In dim Atlantic forests' fold,
The marble wasteth to a crust,
The granite crumbles into mould;
O'er these—left nameless from of old—
As over Shinar's brick and slime,
One vast forgetfulness is roll'd—
Where are the cities of old time?

The lapse of ages, and the rust,
The fire, the frost, the waters cold,
Efface the evil and the just;
From Thebes, that Eriphyle sold,
To drown'd Caer-Is, whose sweet bells toll'd
Beneath the wave a dreamy chime
That echo'd from the mountain-hold,—
"Where are the cities of old time?"

ENVOY.

Prince, all thy towns and cities must
Decay as these, till all their crime,
And mirth, and wealth, and toil are thrust
Where are the cities of old time.

BALLADE OF THE ROYAL GAME OF GOLF.

(EAST FIFESHIRE.)

There are laddies will drive ye a ba'
To the burn frae the farthermost tee,
But ye mauna think driving is a',
Ye may heel her, and send her ajee,
Ye may land in the sand or the sea;
And ye're dune, sir, ye're no worth a preen,
Tak' the word that an auld man 'll gie,
Tak' aye tent to be up on the green!

The auld folk are crouse, and they craw
That their putting is pawky and slee;
In a bunker they're nae gude ava',

But to girn, and to gar the sand flee.
And a lassie can putt—ony she,—
Be she Maggy, or Bessie, or Jean,
But a cleek-shot's the billy for me,
Tak' aye tent to be up on the green!

I hae play'd in the frost and the thaw,
I hae play'd since the year thirty-three,
I hae play'd in the rain and the snaw,
And I trust I may play till I dee;
And I tell ye the truth and nae lee,
For I speak o' the thing I hae seen—
Tom Morris, I ken, will agree—
Tak' aye tent to be up on the green!

ENVOY.

Prince, faith you're improving a wee,
And, Lord, man, they tell me you're keen;
Tak' the best o' advice that can be,
Tak' aye tent to be up on the green!

DOUBLE BALLADE OF PRIMITIVE MAN.

TO J. A. FARRER.

He lived in a cave by the seas,
He lived upon oysters and foes,
But his list of forbidden degrees,
An extensive morality shows;
Geological evidence goes
To prove he had never a pan,
But he shaved with a shell when he chose,—
'Twas the manner of Primitive Man.

He worshipp'd the rain and the breeze,
He worshipp'd the river that flows,
And the Dawn, and the Moon, and the trees,
And bogies, and serpents, and crows;
He buried his dead with their toes
Tucked-up, an original plan,
Till their knees came right under their nose,—
'Twas the manner of Primitive Man.

His communal wives, at his ease,
He would curb with occasional blows;
Or his State had a queen, like the bees

(As another philosopher trows):
When he spoke, it was never in prose,
But he sang in a strain that would scan,
For (to doubt it, perchance, were morose)
'Twas the manner of Primitive Man!

On the coasts that incessantly freeze,
With his stones, and his bones, and his bows;
On luxuriant tropical leas,
Where the summer eternally glows,
He is found, and his habits disclose
(Let theology say what she can)
That he lived in the long, long agos,
'Twas the manner of Primitive Man!

From a status like that of the Crees,
Our society's fabric arose,—
Develop'd, evolved, if you please,
But deluded chronologists chose,
In a fancied accordance with Moses, 4000 B.C. for the span
When he rushed on the world and its woes,—
'Twas the manner of Primitive Man!

But the mild anthropologist,—*he's*
Not *recent* inclined to suppose
Flints Palæolithic like these,
Quaternary bones such as those!
In Rhinoceros, Mammoth and Co.'s,
First epoch, the Human began,
Theologians all to expose,—
'Tis the *mission* of Primitive Man.

ENVOY.

MAX, proudly your Aryans pose,
But their rigs they undoubtedly ran,
For, as every Darwinian knows,
'Twas the manner of Primitive Man! [46]

BALLADE OF AUTUMN.

We built a castle in the air,
In summer weather, you and I,
The wind and sun were in your hair,—
Gold hair against a sapphire sky:
When Autumn came, with leaves that fly

Before the storm, across the plain,
You fled from me, with scarce a sigh—
My Love returns no more again!

The windy lights of Autumn flare:
I watch the moonlit sails go by;
I marvel how men toil and fare,
The weary business that they ply!
Their voyaging is vanity,
And fairy gold is all their gain,
And all the winds of winter cry,
"My Love returns no more again!"

Here, in my castle of Despair,
I sit alone with memory;
The wind-fed wolf has left his lair,
To keep the outcast company.
The brooding owl he hoots hard by,
The hare shall kindle on thy hearth-stane,
The Rhymer's soothest prophecy,—[48]
My Love returns no more again!

ENVOY.

Lady, my home until I die
Is here, where youth and hope were slain;
They flit, the ghosts of our July,
My Love returns no more again!

BALLADE OF TRUE WISDOM.

While others are asking for beauty or fame,
Or praying to know that for which they should pray,
Or courting Queen Venus, that affable dame,
Or chasing the Muses the weary and grey,
The sage has found out a more excellent way—
To Pan and to Pallas his incense he showers,
And his humble petition puts up day by day,
For a house full of books, and a garden of flowers.

Inventors may bow to the God that is lame,
And crave from the fire on his stithy a ray;
Philosophers kneel to the God without name,
Like the people of Athens, agnostics are they;
The hunter a fawn to Diana will slay,
The maiden wild roses will wreathe for the Hours;

But the wise man will ask, ere libation he pay,
For a house full of books, and a garden of flowers.

Oh! grant me a life without pleasure or blame
(As mortals count pleasure who rush through their day
With a speed to which that of the tempest is tame)!
O grant me a house by the beach of a bay,
Where the waves can be surly in winter, and play
With the sea-weed in summer, ye bountiful powers!
And I'd leave all the hurry, the noise, and the fray,
For a house full of books, and a garden of flowers.

ENVOY.

Gods, grant or withhold it; your "yea" and your "nay"
Are immutable, heedless of outcry of ours:
But life *is* worth living, and here we would stay
For a house full of books, and a garden of flowers.

BALLADE OF WORLDLY WEALTH.

(OLD FRENCH.)

Money taketh town and wall,
Fort and ramp without a blow;
Money moves the merchants all,
While the tides shall ebb and flow;
Money maketh Evil show
Like the Good, and Truth like lies:
These alone can ne'er bestow
Youth, and health, and Paradise.

Money maketh festival,
Wine she buys, and beds can strow;
Round the necks of captains tall,
Money wins them chains to throw,
Marches soldiers to and fro,
Gaineth ladies with sweet eyes:
These alone can ne'er bestow
Youth, and health, and Paradise.

Money wins the priest his stall;
Money mitres buys, I trow,
Red hats for the Cardinal,
Abbeys for the novice low;
Money maketh sin as snow,
Place of penitence supplies:

These alone can ne'er bestow
Youth, and health, and Paradise.

BALLADE OF LIFE.

"'Dead and gone,'—a sorry burden of the Ballad of Life."

Death's Jest Book.

Say, fair maids, maying
In gardens green,
In deep dells straying,
What end hath been
Two Mays between
Of the flowers that shone
And your own sweet queen—
"They are dead and gone!"

Say, grave priests, praying
In dule and teen,
From cells decaying
What have ye seen
Of the proud and mean,
Of Judas and John,
Of the foul and clean?—
"They are dead and gone!"

Say, kings, arraying
Loud wars to win,
Of your manslaying
What gain ye glean?
"They are fierce and keen,
But they fall anon,
On the sword that lean,—
They are dead and gone!"

ENVOY.

Through the mad world's scene,
We are drifting on,
To this tune, I ween,
"They are dead and gone!"

BALLADE OF BLUE CHINA.

There's a joy without canker or cark,
There's a pleasure eternally new,
'Tis to gloat on the glaze and the mark

Of china that's ancient and blue;
Unchipp'd all the centuries through
It has pass'd, since the chime of it rang,
And they fashion'd it, figure and hue,
In the reign of the Emperor Hwang.

These dragons (their tails, you remark,
Into bunches of gillyflowers grew),—
When Noah came out of the ark,
Did these lie in wait for his crew?
They snorted, they snapp'd, and they slew,
They were mighty of fin and of fang,
And their portraits Celestials drew
In the reign of the Emperor Hwang.

Here's a pot with a cot in a park,
In a park where the peach-blossoms blew,
Where the lovers eloped in the dark,
Lived, died, and were changed into two
Bright birds that eternally flew
Through the boughs of the may, as they sang:
'Tis a tale was undoubtedly true
In the reign of the Emperor Hwang.

ENVOY.

Come, snarl at my ecstasies, do,
Kind critic, your "tongue has a tang"
But—a sage never heeded a shrew
In the reign of the Emperor Hwang.

BALLADE OF DEAD LADIES.

(AFTER VILLON.)

Nay, tell me now in what strange air
The Roman Flora dwells to-day.
Where Archippiada hides, and where
Beautiful Thais has passed away?
Whence answers Echo, afield, astray,
By mere or stream,—around, below?
Lovelier she than a woman of clay;
Nay, but where is the last year's snow?

Where is wise Héloïse, that care
Brought on Abeilard, and dismay?
All for her love he found a snare,

A maimed poor monk in orders grey;
And where's the Queen who willed to slay
Buridan, that in a sack must go
Afloat down Seine,—a perilous way—
Nay, but where is the last year's snow?

Where's that White Queen, a lily rare,
With her sweet song, the Siren's lay?
Where's Bertha Broad-foot, Beatrice fair?
Alys and Ermengarde, where are they?
Good Joan, whom English did betray
In Rouen town, and burned her? No,
Maiden and Queen, no man may say;
Nay, but where is the last year's snow?

ENVOY.

Prince, all this week thou need'st not pray,
Nor yet this year the thing to know.
One burden answers, ever and aye,
"Nay, but where is the last year's snow?"

VILLON'S BALLADE
OF GOOD COUNSEL, TO HIS FRIENDS OF EVIL LIFE.

Nay, be you pardoner or cheat,
Or cogger keen, or mumper shy,
You'll burn your fingers at the feat,
And howl like other folks that fry.
All evil folks that love a lie!
And where goes gain that greed amasses,
By wile, and trick, and thievery?
'Tis all to taverns and to lasses!

Rhyme, rail, dance, play the cymbals sweet,
With game, and shame, and jollity,
Go jigging through the field and street,
With *myst'ry* and *morality*;
Win gold at *gleek*,—and that will fly,
Where all you gain at *passage* passes,—
And that's? You know as well as I,
'Tis all to taverns and to lasses!

Nay, forth from all such filth retreat,
Go delve and ditch, in wet or dry,
Turn groom, give horse and mule their meat,
If you've no clerkly skill to ply;

You'll gain enough, with husbandry,
But—sow hempseed and such wild grasses,
And where goes all you take thereby?—
'Tis all to taverns and to lasses!

ENVOY.

Your clothes, your hose, your broidery,
Your linen that the snow surpasses,
Or ere they're worn, off, off they fly,
'Tis all to taverns and to lasses!

BALLADE OF THE BOOKWORM.

Far in the Past I peer, and see
A Child upon the Nursery floor,
A Child with books upon his knee,
Who asks, like Oliver, for more!
The number of his years is IV,
And yet in Letters hath he skill,
How deep he dives in Fairy-lore!
The Books I loved, I love them still!

One gift the Fairies gave me: (Three
They commonly bestowed of yore)
The Love of Books, the Golden Key
That opens the Enchanted Door;
Behind it BLUEBEARD lurks, and o'er
And o'er doth JACK his Giants kill,
And there is all ALADDIN'S store,—
The Books I loved, I love them still!

Take all, but leave my Books to me!
These heavy creels of old we bore
We fill not now, nor wander free,
Nor wear the heart that once we wore;
Not now each River seems to pour
His waters from the Muses' hill;
Though something's gone from stream and shore,
The Books I loved, I love them still!

ENVOY.

Fate, that art Queen by shore and sea,
We bow submissive to thy will,
Ah grant, by some benign decree,
The Books I loved—to love them still.

VALENTINE IN FORM OF BALLADE.

The soft wind from the south land sped,
He set his strength to blow,
From forests where Adonis bled,
And lily flowers a-row:
He crossed the straits like streams that flow,
The ocean dark as wine,
To my true love to whisper low,
To be your Valentine.

The Spring half-raised her drowsy head,
Besprent with drifted snow,
"I'll send an April day," she said,
"To lands of wintry woe."
He came,—the winter's overthrow
With showers that sing and shine,
Pied daisies round your path to strow,
To be your Valentine.

Where sands of Egypt, swart and red,
'Neath suns Egyptian glow,
In places of the princely dead,
By the Nile's overflow,
The swallow preened her wings to go,
And for the North did pine,
And fain would brave the frost her foe,
To be your Valentine.

ENVOY.

Spring, Swallow, South Wind, even so,
Their various voice combine;
But that they crave on *me* bestow,
To be your Valentine.

BALLADE OF OLD PLAYS.

(Les Œuvres de Monsieur Molière. A Paris,
chez Louys Billaine, à la Palme.
M.D.C. LXVI.)

LA COUR.

When these Old Plays were new, the King,
Beside the Cardinal's chair,
Applauded, 'mid the courtly ring,
The verses of Molière;

Point-lace was then the only wear,
Old Corneille came to woo,
And bright Du Parc was young and fair,
When these Old Plays were new!

LA COMÉDIE.

How shrill the butcher's cat-calls ring,
How loud the lackeys swear!
Black pipe-bowls on the stage they fling,
At Brécourt, fuming there!
The Porter's stabbed! a Mousquetaire
Breaks in with noisy crew—
'Twas all a commonplace affair
When these Old Plays were new!

LA VILLE.

When these Old Plays were new! They bring
A host of phantoms rare:
Old jests that float, old jibes that sting,
Old faces peaked with care:
Ménage's smirk, de Visé's stare,
The thefts of Jean Ribou,—[66]
Ah, publishers were hard to bear
When these Old Plays were new.

ENVOY.

Ghosts, at your Poet's word ye dare
To break Death's dungeons through,
And frisk, as in that golden air,
When these Old Plays were new!

BALLADE OF HIS BOOKS.

Here stand my books, line upon line
They reach the roof, and row by row,
They speak of faded tastes of mine,
And things I did, but do not, know:
Old school books, useless long ago,
Old Logics, where the spirit, railed in,
Could scarcely answer "yes" or "no"—
The many things I've tried and failed in!

Here's Villon, in morocco fine,
(The Poet starved, in mud and snow,)
Glatigny does not crave to dine,

And René's tears forget to flow.
And here's a work by Mrs. Crowe,
With hosts of ghosts and bogies jailed in;
Ah, all my ghosts have gone below—
The many things I've tried and failed in!

He's touched, this mouldy Greek divine,
The Princess D'Este's hand of snow;
And here the arms of D'Hoym shine,
And there's a tear-bestained Rousseau:
Here's Carlyle shrieking "woe on woe"
(The first edition, this, he wailed in);
I once believed in him—but oh,
The many things I've tried and failed in!

ENVOY.

Prince, tastes may differ; mine and thine
Quite other balances are scaled in;
May you succeed, though I repine—
"The many things I've tried and failed in!"

BALLADE OF THE DREAM.

Swift as sound of music fled
When no more the organ sighs,
Sped as all old days are sped,
So your lips, love, and your eyes,
So your gentle-voiced replies
Mine one hour in sleep that seem,
Rise and flit when slumber flies,
Following darkness like a dream!

Like the scent from roses red,
Like the dawn from golden skies,
Like the semblance of the dead
From the living love that hies,
Like the shifting shade that lies
On the moonlight-silvered stream,
So you rise when dreams arise,
Following darkness like a dream!

Could some spell, or sung or said,
Could some kindly witch and wise,
Lull for aye this dreaming head
In a mist of memories,
I would lie like him who lies

Where the lights on Latmos gleam,—
Wake not, find not Paradise
Following darkness like a dream!

ENVOY.

Sleep, that giv'st what Life denies,
Shadowy bounties and supreme,
Bring the dearest face that flies
Following darkness like a dream!

BALLADE OF THE SOUTHERN CROSS.

Fair islands of the silver fleece,
Hoards of unsunned, uncounted gold,
Whose havens are the haunts of Peace,
Whose boys are in our quarrel bold;
Our bolt is shot, our tale is told,
Our ship of state in storms may toss,
But ye are young if we are old,
Ye Islands of the Southern Cross!

Ay, *we* must dwindle and decrease,
Such fates the ruthless years unfold;
And yet we shall not wholly cease,
We shall not perish unconsoled;
Nay, still shall Freedom keep her hold
Within the sea's inviolate fosse,
And boast her sons of English mould,
Ye Islands of the Southern Cross!

All empires tumble—Rome and Greece—
Their swords are rust, their altars cold!
For us, the Children of the Seas,
Who ruled where'er the waves have rolled,
For us, in Fortune's books enscrolled,
I read no runes of hopeless loss;
Nor—while *ye* last—our knell is tolled,
Ye Islands of the Southern Cross!

ENVOY.

Britannia, when thy hearth's a-cold,
When o'er thy grave has grown the moss,
Still *Rule Australia* shall be trolled
In Islands of the Southern Cross!

BALLADE OF AUCASSIN

Where smooth the southern waters run
By rustling leagues of poplars grey,
Beneath a veiled soft southern sun,
We wandered out of yesterday,
Went maying through that ancient May
Whose fallen flowers are fragrant yet,
And loitered by the fountain spray
With Aucassin and Nicolette.

The grass-grown paths are trod of none
Where through the woods they went astray.
The spider's traceries are spun
Across the darkling forest way.
There come no knights that ride to slay,
No pilgrims through the grasses wet,
No shepherd lads that sang their say
With Aucassin and Nicolette!

'Twas here by Nicolette begun
Her bower of boughs and grasses gay;
'Scaped from the cell of marble dun
'Twas here the lover found the fay,
Ah, lovers fond! ah, foolish play!
How hard we find it to forget
Who fain would dwell with them as they,
With Aucassin and Nicolette.

ENVOY.

Prince, 'tis a melancholy lay!
For youth, for love we both regret.
How fair they seem, how far away,
With Aucassin and Nicolette!

BALLADE AMOUREUSE.

AFTER FROISSART.

Not Jason nor Medea wise,
I crave to see, nor win much lore,
Nor list to Orpheus' minstrelsies;
Nor Her'cles would I see, that o'er
The wide world roamed from shore to shore;
Nor, by St. James, Penelope,—
Nor pure Lucrece, such wrong that bore:
To see my Love suffices me!

Virgil and Cato, no man vies
With them in wealth of clerkly store;
I would not see them with mine eyes;
Nor him that sailed, *sans* sail nor oar,
Across the barren sea and hoar,
And all for love of his ladye;
Nor pearl nor sapphire takes me more:
To see my Love suffices me!

I heed not Pegasus, that flies
As swift as shafts the bowmen pour;
Nor famed Pygmalion's artifice,
Whereof the like was ne'er before;
Nor Oléus, that drank of yore
The salt wave of the whole great sea:
Why? dost thou ask? 'Tis as I swore—
To see my Love suffices me!

BALLADE OF QUEEN ANNE.

The modish Airs,
The Tansey Brew,
The *Swains* and *Fairs*
In curtained Pew;
Nymphs KNELLER drew,
Books BENTLEY read,—
Who knows them, who?
QUEEN ANNE is dead!

We buy her Chairs,
Her China blue,
Her red-brick Squares
We build anew;
But ah! we rue,
When all is said,
The tale o'er-true,
QUEEN ANNE is dead!

Now *Bulls* and *Bears*,
A ruffling Crew,
With Stocks and Shares,
With Turk and Jew,
Go bubbling through
The Town ill-bred:
The World's askew,
QUEEN ANNE is dead!

ENVOY.

> Friend, praise the new;
> The old is fled:
> *Vivat* FROU-FROU!
> QUEEN ANNE is dead!

BALLADE OF BLIND LOVE.

(AFTER LYONNET DE COISMES.)

> Who have loved and ceased to love, forget
> That ever they loved in their lives, they say;
> Only remember the fever and fret,
> And the pain of Love, that was all his pay;
> All the delight of him passes away
> From hearts that hoped, and from lips that met—
> Too late did I love you, my love, and yet
> I shall never forget till my dying day.
>
> Too late were we 'ware of the secret net
> That meshes the feet in the flowers that stray;
> There were we taken and snared, Lisette,
> In the dungeon of **La Fausse Amistié**;
> Help was there none in the wide world's fray,
> Joy was there none in the gift and the debt;
> Too late we knew it, too long regret—
> I shall never forget till my dying day!
>
> We must live our lives, though the sun be set,
> Must meet in the masque where parts we play,
> Must cross in the maze of Life's minuet;
> Our yea is yea, and our nay is nay:
> But while snows of winter or flowers of May
> Are the sad year's shroud or coronet,
> In the season of rose or of violet,
> I shall never forget till my dying day!

ENVOY.

> Queen, when the clay is my coverlet,
> When I am dead, and when you are grey,
> Vow, where the grass of the grave is wet,
> "I shall never forget till my dying day!"

BALLADE OF HIS CHOICE OF A SEPULCHRE.

Here I'd come when weariest!
   Here the breast
Of the Windburg's tufted over
Deep with bracken; here his crest
   Takes the west,
Where the wide-winged hawk doth hover.

Silent here are lark and plover;
   In the cover
Deep below the cushat best
Loves his mate, and croons above her
   O'er their nest,
Where the wide-winged hawk doth hover.

Bring me here, Life's tired-out guest,
   To the blest
Bed that waits the weary rover,
Here should failure be confessed;
   Ends my quest,
Where the wide-winged hawk doth hover!

ENVOY.

Friend, or stranger kind, or lover,
Ah, fulfil a last behest,
   Let me rest
Where the wide-winged hawk doth hover!

DIZAIN.

As, to the pipe, with rhythmic feet
In windings of some old-world dance,
The smiling couples cross and meet,
Join hands, and then in line advance,
So, to these fair old tunes of France,
Through all their maze of to-and-fro,
The light-heeled numbers laughing go,
Retreat, return, and ere they flee,
One moment pause in panting row,
And seem to say—Vos plaudite!

A. D.

VERSES AND TRANSLATIONS.

ORONTE—*Ce ne sont point de ces grands vers pompeux,
Mais de petits vers*!

"Le Misanthrope," Acte i., Sc. 2.

A PORTRAIT OF 1783.

Your hair and chin are like the hair
And chin Burne-Jones's ladies wear;
You were unfashionably fair
   In '83;
And sad you were when girls are gay,
You read a book about *Le vrai
Mérite de l'homme*, alone in May.
What *can* it be,
Le vrai mérite de l'homme? Not gold,
Not titles that are bought and sold,
Not wit that flashes and is cold,
   But Virtue merely!
Instructed by Jean-Jacques Rousseau
(And Jean-Jacques, surely, ought to know),
You bade the crowd of foplings go,
   You glanced severely,
Dreaming beneath the spreading shade
Of 'that vast hat the Graces made;' [88]
So Rouget sang—while yet he played
   With courtly rhyme,
And hymned great Doisi's red perruque,
And Nice's eyes, and Zulmé's look,
And dead canaries, ere he shook
   The sultry time
With strains like thunder. Loud and low
Methinks I hear the murmur grow,
The tramp of men that come and go
   With fire and sword.
They war against the quick and dead,
Their flying feet are dashed with red,
As theirs the vintaging that tread
   Before the Lord.
O head unfashionably fair,
What end was thine, for all thy care?

We only see thee dreaming there:
   We cannot see
The breaking of thy vision, when
The Rights of Man were lords of men,
When virtue won her own again
   In '93.

THE MOON'S MINION.

(FROM THE PROSE OF C. BAUDELAIRE.)

Thine eyes are like the sea, my dear,
   The wand'ring waters, green and grey;
Thine eyes are wonderful and clear,
   And deep, and deadly, even as they;
The spirit of the changeful sea
   Informs thine eyes at night and noon,
She sways the tides, and the heart of thee,
   The mystic, sad, capricious Moon!

The Moon came down the shining stair
   Of clouds that fleck the summer sky,
She kissed thee, saying, "Child, be fair,
   And madden men's hearts, even as I;
Thou shalt love all things strange and sweet,
   That know me and are known of me;
The lover thou shalt never meet,
   The land where thou shalt never be!"

She held thee in her chill embrace,
   She kissed thee with cold lips divine,
She left her pallor on thy face,
   That mystic ivory face of thine;
And now I sit beside thy feet,
   And all my heart is far from thee,
Dreaming of her I shall not meet,
   And of the land I shall not see!

IN ITHACA.

> "And now am I greatly repenting that ever I left my life with thee, and the immortality thou didst promise me."—*Letter of Odysseus to Calypso.* Luciani *Vera Historia.*

'Tis thought Odysseus when the strife was o'er
   With all the waves and wars, a weary while,
   Grew restless in his disenchanted isle,

And still would watch the sunset, from the shore,
Go down the ways of gold, and evermore
   His sad heart followed after, mile on mile,
   Back to the Goddess of the magic wile,
Calypso, and the love that was of yore.

Thou too, thy haven gained, must turn thee yet
   To look across the sad and stormy space,
   Years of a youth as bitter as the sea,
Ah, with a heavy heart, and eyelids wet,
   Because, within a fair forsaken place
   The life that might have been is lost to thee.

HOMER.

Homer, thy song men liken to the sea
   With all the notes of music in its tone,
   With tides that wash the dim dominion
Of Hades, and light waves that laugh in glee
Around the isles enchanted; nay, to me
   Thy verse seems as the River of source unknown
   That glasses Egypt's temples overthrown
In his sky-nurtured stream, eternally.

No wiser we than men of heretofore
   To find thy sacred fountains guarded fast;
Enough, thy flood makes green our human shore,
   As Nilus Egypt, rolling down his vast
His fertile flood, that murmurs evermore
   Of gods dethroned, and empires in the past.

THE BURIAL OF MOLIÈRE.

(AFTER J. TRUFFIER.)

Dead—he is dead! The rouge has left a trace
   On that thin cheek where shone, perchance, a tear,
   Even while the people laughed that held him dear
But yesterday. He died,—and not in grace,
And many a black-robed caitiff starts apace
   To slander him whose *Tartuffe* made them fear,
   And gold must win a passage for his bier,
And bribe the crowd that guards his resting-place.

Ah, Molière, for that last time of all,
   Man's hatred broke upon thee, and went by,
And did but make more fair thy funeral.

Though in the dark they hid thee stealthily,
Thy coffin had the cope of night for pall,
  For torch, the stars along the windy sky!

BION.

The wail of Moschus on the mountains crying
  The Muses heard, and loved it long ago;
They heard the hollows of the hills replying,
  They heard the weeping water's overflow;
They winged the sacred strain—the song undying,
  The song that all about the world must go,—
When poets for a poet dead are sighing,
  The minstrels for a minstrel friend laid low.

And dirge to dirge that answers, and the weeping
  For Adonais by the summer sea,
The plaints for Lycidas, and Thyrsis (sleeping
  Far from 'the forest ground called Thessaly'),
These hold thy memory, Bion, in their keeping,
  And are but echoes of the moan for thee.

SPRING.

(AFTER MELEAGER.)

Now the bright crocus flames, and now
  The slim narcissus takes the rain,
And, straying o'er the mountain's brow,
  The daffodilies bud again.
  The thousand blossoms wax and wane
On wold, and heath, and fragrant bough,
But fairer than the flowers art thou,
  Than any growth of hill or plain.

Ye gardens, cast your leafy crown,
That my Love's feet may tread it down,
  Like lilies on the lilies set;
My Love, whose lips are softer far
Than drowsy poppy petals are,
  And sweeter than the violet!

BEFORE THE SNOW.

(AFTER ALBERT GLATIGNY.)

The winter is upon us, not the snow,
  The hills are etched on the horizon bare,

    The skies are iron grey, a bitter air,
The meagre cloudlets shudder to and fro.
One yellow leaf the listless wind doth blow,
    Like some strange butterfly, unclassed and rare.
    Your footsteps ring in frozen alleys, where
The black trees seem to shiver as you go.

Beyond lie church and steeple, with their old
    And rusty vanes that rattle as they veer,
A sharper gust would shake them from their hold,
    Yet up that path, in summer of the year,
And past that melancholy pile we strolled
    To pluck wild strawberries, with merry cheer.

VILLANELLE.

TO LUCIA.

Apollo left the golden Muse
    And shepherded a mortal's sheep,
Theocritus of Syracuse!

To mock the giant swain that woo's
    The sea-nymph in the sunny deep,
Apollo left the golden Muse.

Afield he drove his lambs and ewes,
    Where Milon and where Battus reap,
Theocritus of Syracuse!

To watch thy tunny-fishers cruise
    Below the dim Sicilian steep
Apollo left the golden Muse.

Ye twain did loiter in the dews,
    Ye slept the swain's unfever'd sleep,
Theocritus of Syracuse!

That Time might half with *his* confuse
    Thy songs,—like his, that laugh and leap,—
Theocritus of Syracuse,
    Apollo left the golden Muse!

NATURAL THEOLOGY.

    ἐπεὶ καὶ τοῦτον ὀΐομαι ἀθανάτοισιν
εὔχεσθαι·. Πάντες δὲ θεῶν χατέουσ' ἄνθρωποι.

OD. III. 47.

"Once CAGN was like a father, kind and good,
  But He was spoiled by fighting many things;
He wars upon the lions in the wood,
  And breaks the Thunder-bird's tremendous wings;
But still we cry to Him,—*We are thy brood*—
  O Cagn, be merciful! and us He brings
To herds of elands, and great store of food,
  And in the desert opens water-springs."

So Qing, King Nqsha's Bushman hunter, spoke,
  Beside the camp-fire, by the fountain fair,
When all were weary, and soft clouds of smoke
  Were fading, fragrant, in the twilit air:
And suddenly in each man's heart there woke
  A pang, a sacred memory of prayer.

THE ODYSSEY.

As one that for a weary space has lain
  Lulled by the song of Circe and her wine
  In gardens near the pale of Proserpine,
Where that Ææan isle forgets the main,
And only the low lutes of love complain,
  And only shadows of wan lovers pine,
  As such an one were glad to know the brine
Salt on his lips, and the large air again,—
So gladly, from the songs of modern speech
  Men turn, and see the stars, and feel the free
    Shrill wind beyond the close of heavy flowers,
    And through the music of the languid hours,
They hear like ocean on a western beach
  The surge and thunder of the Odyssey.

IDEAL.

Suggested by a female head in wax, of unknown date, but supposed to be either of the best Greek age, or a work of Raphael or Leonardo. It is now in the Lille Museum.

Ah, mystic child of Beauty, nameless maid,
  Dateless and fatherless, how long ago,
A Greek, with some rare sadness overweighed,
  Shaped thee, perchance, and quite forgot his woe!
  Or Raphael thy sweetness did bestow,
While magical his fingers o'er thee strayed,
  Or that great pupil taught of Verrocchio
Redeemed thy still perfection from the shade

That hides all fair things lost, and things unborn,
   Where one has fled from me, that wore thy grace,
   And that grave tenderness of thine awhile;
Nay, still in dreams I see her, but her face
   Is pale, is wasted with a touch of scorn,
   And only on thy lips I find her smile.

THE FAIRY'S GIFT.

"Take short views."—SYDNEY SMITH.

The Fays that to my christ'ning came
   (For come they did, my nurses taught me),
They did not bring me wealth or fame,
   'Tis very little that they brought me.
But one, the crossest of the crew,
   The ugly old one, uninvited,
Said, "I shall be avenged on *you*,
   My child; you shall grow up short-sighted!"
With magic juices did she lave
   Mine eyes, and wrought her wicked pleasure.
Well, of all gifts the Fairies gave,
   Hers is the present that I treasure!

The bore whom others fear and flee,
   I do not fear, I do not flee him;
I pass him calm as calm can be;
   I do not cut—I do not see him!
And with my feeble eyes and dim,
   Where *you* see patchy fields and fences,
For me the mists of Turner swim—
   My "azure distance" soon commences!
Nay, as I blink about the streets
   Of this befogged and miry city,
Why, almost every girl one meets
   Seems preternaturally pretty!
"Try spectacles," one's friends intone;
   "You'll see the world correctly through them."
But I have visions of my own,
   And not for worlds would I undo them.

BENEDETTA RAMUS.

AFTER ROMNEY.

   Mysterious Benedetta! who
   That Reynolds or that Romney drew

Was ever half so fair as you,
   Or is so well forgot?
These eyes of melancholy brown,
These woven locks, a shadowy crown,
Must surely have bewitched the town;
   Yet you're remembered not.

Through all that prattle of your age,
Through lore of fribble and of sage
I've read, and chiefly Walpole's page,
   Wherein are beauties famous;
I've haunted ball, and rout, and sale;
I've heard of Devonshire and Thrale,
And all the Gunnings' wondrous tale,
   But nothing of Miss Ramus.

And yet on many a lattice pane
'Fair Benedetta,' scrawled in vain
By lovers' diamonds, must remain
   To tell us you were cruel. [108]
But who, of all that sighed and swore—
Wits, poets, courtiers by the score—
Did win and on his bosom wore
   This hard and lovely jewel?

Why, dilettante records say
An Alderman, who came that way,
Woo'd you and made you Lady Day;
   You crowned his civic flame.
It suits a melancholy song
To think your heart had suffered wrong,
And that you lived not very long
   To be a City dame!

Perchance you were a Mourning Bride,
And conscious of a heart that died
With one who fell by Rodney's side
   In blood-stained Spanish bays.
Perchance 'twas no such thing, and you
Dwelt happy with your knight and true,
And, like Aurora, watched a crew
   Of rosy little Days!

Oh, lovely face and innocent!
Whatever way your fortunes went,
And if to earth your life was lent

For little space or long,
In your kind eyes we seem to see
What Woman at her best may be,
And offer to your memory
   An unavailing song!

PARTANT POUR LA SCRIBIE.

[Scribie, on the north-east littoral of Bohemia, is the land of stage conventions. It is named after the discoverer, M. Scribe.]

A pleasant land is Scribie, where
   The light comes mostly from below,
And seems a sort of symbol rare
   Of things at large, and how they go,
In rooms where doors are everywhere
   And cupboards shelter friend or foe.

This is a realm where people tell
   Each other, when they chance to meet,
Of things that long ago befell—
   And do most solemnly repeat
Secrets they both know very well,
   Aloud, and in the public street!

A land where lovers go in fours,
   Master and mistress, man and maid;
Where people listen at the doors
   Or 'neath a table's friendly shade,
And comic Irishmen in scores
   Roam o'er the scenes all undismayed:

A land where Virtue in distress
   Owes much to uncles in disguise;
Where British sailors frankly bless
   Their limbs, their timbers, and their eyes;
And where the villain doth confess,
   Conveniently, before he dies!

A land of lovers false and gay;
   A land where people dread a "curse;"
A land of letters gone astray,
   Or intercepted, which is worse;
Where weddings false fond maids betray,
   And all the babes are changed at nurse.

Oh, happy land, where things come right!
   We of the world where things go ill;
Where lovers love, but don't unite;
   Where no one finds the Missing Will—
Dominion of the heart's delight,
   Scribie, we've loved, and love thee still!

ST. ANDREW'S BAY.

NIGHT.

Ah, listen through the music, from the shore,
The "melancholy long-withdrawing roar";
Beneath the Minster, and the windy caves,
The wide North Ocean, marshalling his waves
Even so forlorn—in worlds beyond our ken—
May sigh the seas that are not heard of men;
Even so forlorn, prophetic of man's fate,
Sounded the cold sea-wave disconsolate,
When none but God might hear the boding tone,
As God shall hear the long lament alone,
When all is done, when all the tale is told,
And the gray sea-wave echoes as of old!

MORNING.

This was the burden of the Night,
   The saying of the sea,
But lo! the hours have brought the light,
The laughter of the waves, the flight
Of dipping sea-birds, foamy white,
   That are so glad to be!
"Forget!" the happy creatures cry,
   "Forget Night's monotone,
With us be glad in sea and sky,
The days are thine, the days that fly,
The days God gives to know him by,
   And not the Night alone!"

WOMAN AND THE WEED.

(FOUNDED ON A NEW ZEALAND MYTH.)

In the Morning of Time, when his fortunes began,
How bleak, how un-Greek, was the Nature of Man!
From his wigwam, if ever he ventured to roam,
There was nobody waiting to welcome him home;

For the Man had been made, but the woman had *not*,
And Earth was a highly detestable spot.
Man hated his neighbours; they met and they scowled,
They did not converse but they struggled and howled,
For Man had no tact—he would ne'er take a hint,
And his notions he backed with a hatchet of flint.

So Man was alone, and he wished he could see
On the Earth some one like him, but fairer than he,
With locks like the red gold, a smile like the sun,
To welcome him back when his hunting was done.
And he sighed for a voice that should answer him still,
Like the affable Echo he heard on the hill:
That should answer him softly and always agree,
And oh, Man reflected, *how nice it would be*!

So he prayed to the Gods, and they stooped to his prayer,
And they spoke to the Sun on his way through the air,
And he married the Echo one fortunate morn,
And Woman, their beautiful daughter, was born!
The daughter of Sunshine and Echo she came
With a voice like a song, with a face like a flame;
With a face like a flame, and a voice like a song,
And happy was Man, but it was not for long!

For weather's a painfully changeable thing,
Not always the child of the Echo would sing;
And the face of the Sun may be hidden with mist,
And his child can be terribly cross if she list.
And unfortunate Man had to learn with surprise
That a frown's not peculiar to masculine eyes;
That the sweetest of voices can scold and can sneer,
And cannot be answered—like men—with a spear.

So Man went and called to the Gods in his woe,
And they answered him—"Sir, you would needs have it so:
And the thing must go on as the thing has begun,
She's immortal—your child of the Echo and Sun.
But we'll send you another, and fairer is she,
This maiden with locks that are flowing and free.
This maiden so gentle, so kind, and so fair,
With a flower like a star in the night of her hair.
With her eyes like the smoke that is misty and blue,
With her heart that is heavenly, and tender, and true.
She will die in the night, but no need you should mourn,

- 42 -

You shall bury her body and thence shall be born
A weed that is green, that is fragrant and fair,
With a flower like the star in the night of her hair.
And the leaves must ye burn till they offer to you
Soft smoke, like her eyes that are misty and blue.

"And the smoke shall ye breathe and no more shall ye fret,
But the child of the Echo and Sun shall forget:
Shall forget all the trouble and torment she brings,
Shall bethink ye of none but delectable things;
And the sound of the wars with your brethren shall cease,
While ye smoke by the camp-fire the great pipe of peace."
So the last state of Man was by no means the worst,
The second gift softened the sting of the first.

Nor the child of the Echo and Sun doth he heed
When he dreams with the Maid that was changed to the weed;
Though the Echo be silent, the Sun in a mist,
The Maid is the fairest that ever was kissed.
And when tempests are over and ended the rain,
And the child of the Sunshine is sunny again,
He comes back, glad at heart, and again is at one
With the changeable child of the Echo and Sun.

RHYMES À LA MODE

BALLADE DEDICATORY,
TO
MRS. ELTON
OF WHITE STAUNTON.

THE painted Briton built his mound,
And left his celts and clay,
On yon fair slope of sunlit ground
That fronts your garden gay;
The Roman came, he bore the sway,
He bullied, bought, and sold,
Your fountain sweeps his works away
Beside your manor old!

But still his crumbling urns are found
Within the window-bay,
Where once he listened to the sound
That lulls you day by day;—
The sound of summer winds at play,
The noise of waters cold
To Yarty wandering on their way,
Beside your manor old!

The Roman fell: his firm-set bound
Became the Saxon's stay;
The bells made music all around
For monks in cloisters grey,
Till fled the monks in disarray
From their warm chantry's fold,
Old Abbots slumber as they may,
Beside your manor old!

ENVOY.

Creeds, empires, peoples, all decay,
Down into darkness, rolled;
May life that's fleet be sweet, I pray,
Beside your manor old.

THE FORTUNATE ISLANDS.
THE FORTUNATE ISLANDS.
A DREAM IN JUNE.

IN twilight of the longest day
   I lingered over Lucian,
Till ere the dawn a dreamy way
   My spirit found, untrod of man,
Between the green sky and the grey.

Amid the soft dusk suddenly
   More light than air I seemed to sail,
Afloat upon the ocean sky,
   While through the faint blue, clear and pale,
I saw the mountain clouds go by:
   My barque had thought for helm and sail,
And one mist wreath for canopy.

Like torches on a marble floor
   Reflected, so the wild stars shone,
Within the abysmal hyaline,
   Till the day widened more and more,
And sank to sunset, and was gone,
And then, as burning beacons shine
   On summits of a mountain isle,
     A light to folk on sea that fare,
   So the sky's beacons for a while
     Burned in these islands of the air.

Then from a starry island set
   Where one swift tide of wind there flows,
Came scent of lily and violet,
   Narcissus, hyacinth, and rose,
Laurel, and myrtle buds, and vine,
So delicate is the air and fine:
And forests of all fragrant trees
   Sloped seaward from the central hill,
And ever clamorous were these
With singing of glad birds; and still
   Such music came as in the woods
Most lonely, consecrate to Pan,
   The Wind makes, in his many moods,
Upon the pipes some shepherd Man,
   Hangs up, in thanks for victory!

On these shall mortals play no more,
   But the Wind doth touch them, over and o'er,
And the Wind's breath in the reeds will sigh.

Between the daylight and the dark
   That island lies in silver air,
And suddenly my magic barque
   Wheeled, and ran in, and grounded there;
And by me stood the sentinel
   Of them who in the island dwell;
     All smiling did he bind my hands,
     With rushes green and rosy bands,
They have no harsher bonds than these
   The people of the pleasant lands
Within the wash of the airy seas!

Then was I to their city led:
   Now all of ivory and gold
The great walls were that garlanded
The temples in their shining fold,
   (Each fane of beryl built, and each
   Girt with its grove of shadowy beech,)
And all about the town, and through,
There flowed a River fed with dew,
   As sweet as roses, and as clear
     As mountain crystals pure and cold,
And with his waves that water kissed
The gleaming altars of amethyst
   That smoke with victims all the year,
And sacred are to the Gods of old.

There sat three Judges by the Gate,
   And I was led before the Three,
And they but looked on me, and straight
   The rosy bonds fell down from me
   Who, being innocent, was free;
And I might wander at my will
About that City on the hill,
   Among the happy people clad
     In purple weeds of woven air
Hued like the webs that Twilight weaves
At shut of languid summer eves
   So light their raiment seemed; and glad
Was every face I looked on there!

There was no heavy heat, no cold,
   The dwellers there wax never old,
     Nor wither with the waning time,
But each man keeps that age he had
     When first he won the fairy clime.
The Night falls never from on high,
   Nor ever burns the heat of noon.
But such soft light eternally
   Shines, as in silver dawns of June
Before the Sun hath climbed the sky!

Within these pleasant streets and wide,
   The souls of Heroes go and come,
Even they that fell on either side
   Beneath the walls of Ilium;
And sunlike in that shadowy isle
The face of Helen and her smile
   Makes glad the souls of them that knew
Grief for her sake a little while!
And all true Greeks and wise are there;
And with his hand upon the hair
   Of Phaedo, saw I Socrates,
About him many youths and fair,
   Hylas, Narcissus, and with these
Him whom the quoit of Phoebus slew
   By fleet Eurotas, unaware!

All these their mirth and pleasure made
   Within the plain Elysian,
     The fairest meadow that may be,
With all green fragrant trees for shade
   And every scented wind to fan,
     And sweetest flowers to strew the lea;
The soft Winds are their servants fleet
   To fetch them every fruit at will
   And water from the river chill;
And every bird that singeth sweet
   Throstle, and merle, and nightingale
   Brings blossoms from the dewy vale,—
Lily, and rose, and asphodel—
   With these doth each guest twine his crown
   And wreathe his cup, and lay him down
     Beside some friend he loveth well.

There with the shining Souls I lay
When, lo, a Voice that seemed to say,
   In far-off haunts of Memory,
Whoso doth taste the Dead Men's bread,
Shall dwell for ever with these Dead,
Nor ever shall his body lie
Beside his friends, on the grey hill
Where rains weep, and the curlews shrill
And the brown water wanders by!

Then did a new soul in me wake,
The dead men's bread I feared to break,
Their fruit I would not taste indeed
Were it but a pomegranate seed.
Nay, not with these I made my choice
To dwell for ever and rejoice,
For otherwhere the River rolls
That girds the home of Christian souls,
And these my whole heart seeks are found
On otherwise enchanted ground.

Even so I put the cup away,
   The vision wavered, dimmed, and broke,
   And, nowise sorrowing, I woke
While, grey among the ruins grey
Chill through the dwellings of the dead,
   The Dawn crept o'er the Northern sea,
Then, in a moment, flushed to red,
   Flushed all the broken minster old,
   And turned the shattered stones to gold,
And wakened half the world with me!

L'Envoi.

To E. W. G.

(Who also had rhymed on the *Fortunate Islands* of Lucian).

Each in the self-same field we glean
The field of the Samosatene,
Each something takes and something leaves
   And this must choose, and that forego
In Lucian's visionary sheaves,
   To twine a modern posy so;
But all my gleanings, truth to tell,
Are mixed with mournful asphodel,

While yours are wreathed with poppies red,
  With flowers that Helen's feet have kissed,
With leaves of vine that garlanded
  The Syrian Pantagruelist,
The sage who laughed the world away,
  Who mocked at Gods, and men, and care,
More sweet of voice than Rabelais,
  And lighter-hearted than Voltaire.

ALMAE MATRES.

ALMAE MATRES.

(ST. ANDREWS, 1862. OXFORD, 1865.)

ST. Andrews by the Northern sea,
  A haunted town it is to me!
A little city, worn and grey,
  The grey North Ocean girds it round.
And o'er the rocks, and up the bay,
  The long sea-rollers surge and sound.
And still the thin and biting spray
  Drives down the melancholy street,
And still endure, and still decay,
  Towers that the salt winds vainly beat.
Ghost-like and shadowy they stand
Dim mirrored in the wet sea-sand.

St. Leonard's chapel, long ago
  We loitered idly where the tall
Fresh budded mountain ashes blow
  Within thy desecrated wall:
The tough roots rent the tomb below,
  The April birds sang clamorous,
We did not dream, we could not know
  How hardly Fate would deal with us!

O, broken minster, looking forth
  Beyond the bay, above the town,
O, winter of the kindly North,
  O, college of the scarlet gown,
And shining sands beside the sea,
  And stretch of links beyond the sand,
Once more I watch you, and to me
  It is as if I touched his hand!

And therefore art thou yet more dear,
    O, little city, grey and sere,
Though shrunken from thine ancient pride
    And lonely by thy lonely sea,
Than these fair halls on Isis' side,
    Where Youth an hour came back to me!

A land of waters green and clear,
    Of willows and of poplars tall,
And, in the spring time of the year,
    The white may breaking over all,
And Pleasure quick to come at call.
    And summer rides by marsh and wold,
And Autumn with her crimson pall
    About the towers of Magdalen rolled;
And strange enchantments from the past,
    And memories of the friends of old,
And strong Tradition, binding fast
    The "flying terms" with bands of gold,—

All these hath Oxford: all are dear,
    But dearer far the little town,
The drifting surf, the wintry year,
    The college of the scarlet gown,
      St. Andrews by the Northern sea,
      That is a haunted town to me!

DESIDERIUM.

IN MEMORIAM S. F. A.

THE call of homing rooks, the shrill
    Song of some bird that watches late,
The cries of children break the still
    Sad twilight by the churchyard gate.

And o'er your far-off tomb the grey
    Sad twilight broods, and from the trees
The rooks call on their homeward way,
    And are you heedless quite of these?

The clustered rowan berries red
    And Autumn's may, the clematis,
They droop above your dreaming head,
    And these, and all things must you miss?

Ah, you that loved the twilight air,
   The dim lit hour of quiet best,
At last, at last you have your share
   Of what life gave so seldom, rest!

Yes, rest beyond all dreaming deep,
   Or labour, nearer the Divine,
And pure from fret, and smooth as sleep,
   And gentle as thy soul, is thine!

So let it be! But could I know
   That thou in this soft autumn eve,
This hush of earth that pleased thee so,
   Hadst pleasure still, I might not grieve.

RHYMES À LA MODE.

BALLADE OF MIDDLE AGE.

OUR youth began with tears and sighs,
With seeking what we could not find;
Our verses all were threnodies,
In elegiacs still we whined;
Our ears were deaf, our eyes were blind,
We sought and knew not what we sought.
We marvel, now we look behind:
Life's more amusing than we thought!

Oh, foolish youth, untimely wise!
Oh, phantoms of the sickly mind!
What? not content with seas and skies,
With rainy clouds and southern wind,
With common cares and faces kind,
With pains and joys each morning brought?
Ah, old, and worn, and tired we find
Life's more amusing than we thought!

Though youth "turns spectre-thin and dies,"
To mourn for youth we're not inclined;
We set our souls on salmon flies,
We whistle where we once repined.
Confound the woes of human-kind!
By Heaven we're "well deceived," I wot;
Who hum, contented or resigned,
"Life's more amusing than we thought"!

ENVOY.

O nate mecum, worn and lined
Our faces show, but that is naught;
Our hearts are young 'neath wrinkled rind:
Life's more amusing than we thought!

THE LAST CAST.

THE ANGLER'S APOLOGY.

JUST one cast more! how many a year
   Beside how many a pool and stream,
Beneath the falling leaves and sere,
   I've sighed, reeled up, and dreamed my dream!

Dreamed of the sport since April first
   Her hands fulfilled of flowers and snow,
Adown the pastoral valleys burst
   Where Ettrick and where Teviot flow.

Dreamed of the singing showers that break,
   And sting the lochs, or near or far,
And rouse the trout, and stir "the take"
   From Urigil to Lochinvar.

Dreamed of the kind propitious sky
   O'er Ari Innes brooding grey;
The sea trout, rushing at the fly,
   Breaks the black wave with sudden spray!

* * * * *

Brief are man's days at best; perchance
   I waste my own, who have not seen
The castled palaces of France
   Shine on the Loire in summer green.

And clear and fleet Eurotas still,
   You tell me, laves his reedy shore,
And flows beneath his fabled hill
   Where Dian drave the chase of yore.

And "like a horse unbroken" yet
   The yellow stream with rush and foam,
'Neath tower, and bridge, and parapet,
   Girdles his ancient mistress, Rome!

I may not see them, but I doubt
   If seen I'd find them half so fair

> As ripples of the rising trout
>   That feed beneath the elms of Yair.
>
> Nay, Spring I'd meet by Tweed or Ail,
>   And Summer by Loch Assynt's deep,
> And Autumn in that lonely vale
>   Where wedded Avons westward sweep,
>
> Or where, amid the empty fields,
>   Among the bracken of the glen,
> Her yellow wreath October yields,
>   To crown the crystal brows of Ken.
>
> Unseen, Eurotas, southward steal,
>   Unknown, Alpheus, westward glide,
> You never heard the ringing reel,
>   The music of the water side!
>
> Though Gods have walked your woods among,
>   Though nymphs have fled your banks along;
> You speak not that familiar tongue
>   Tweed murmurs like my cradle song.
>
> My cradle song,—nor other hymn
>   I'd choose, nor gentler requiem dear
> Than Tweed's, that through death's twilight dim,
>   Mourned in the latest Minstrel's ear!

TWILIGHT.

SONNET.

(AFTER RICHEPIN.)

> LIGHT has flown!
>   Through the grey
>   The wind's way
> The sea's moan
> Sound alone!
>   For the day
>   These repay
> And atone!
>
> Scarce I know,
> Listening so
>   To the streams
>   Of the sea,

If old dreams
Sing to me!

BALLADE OF SUMMER.

TO C. H. ARKCOLL.

WHEN strawberry pottles are common and cheap,
Ere elms be black, or limes be sere,
When midnight dances are murdering sleep,
Then comes in the sweet o' the year!
And far from Fleet Street, far from here,
The Summer is Queen in the length of the land,
And moonlit nights they are soft and clear,
When fans for a penny are sold in the Strand!

When clamour that doves in the lindens keep
Mingles with musical plash of the weir,
Where drowned green tresses of crowsfoot creep,
Then comes in the sweet o' the year!
And better a crust and a beaker of beer,
With rose-hung hedges on either hand,
Than a palace in town and a prince's cheer,
When fans for a penny are sold in the Strand!

When big trout late in the twilight leap,
When cuckoo clamoureth far and near,
When glittering scythes in the hayfield reap,
Then comes in the sweet o' the year!
And it's oh to sail, with the wind to steer,
Where kine knee deep in the water stand,
On a Highland loch, on a Lowland mere,
When fans for a penny are sold in the Strand!

ENVOY.

Friend, with the fops while we dawdle here,
Then comes in the sweet o' the year!
And the Summer runs out, like grains of sand,
When fans for a penny are sold in the Strand!

BALLADE OF CHRISTMAS GHOSTS.

BETWEEN the moonlight and the fire
In winter twilights long ago,
What ghosts we raised for your desire
To make your merry blood run slow!
How old, how grave, how wise we grow!

No Christmas ghost can make us chill,
Save *those* that troop in mournful row,
The ghosts we all can raise at will!

The beasts can talk in barn and byre
On Christmas Eve, old legends know,
As year by year the years retire,
We men fall silent then I trow,
Such sights hath Memory to show,
Such voices from the silence thrill,
Such shapes return with Christmas snow,—
The ghosts we all can raise at will.

Oh, children of the village choir,
Your carols on the midnight throw,
Oh bright across the mist and mire
Ye ruddy hearths of Christmas glow!
Beat back the dread, beat down the woe,
Let's cheerily descend the hill;
Be welcome all, to come or go,
The ghosts we all can raise at will!

ENVOY.

Friend, *sursum corda*, soon or slow
We part, like guests who've joyed their fill;
Forget them not, nor mourn them so,
The ghosts we all can raise at will!

LOVE'S EASTER.

SONNET.

LOVE died here
  Long ago;
O'er his bier,
  Lying low,
  Poppies throw;
    Shed no tear;
    Year by year,
Roses blow!

Year by year,
Adon—dear
  To Love's Queen—
    Does not die!

Wakes when green
  May is nigh!

BALLADE OF THE GIRTON GIRL.

SHE has just "put her gown on" at Girton,
  She is learned in Latin and Greek,
But lawn tennis she plays with a skirt on
  That the prudish remark with a shriek.
In her accents, perhaps, she is weak
  (Ladies *are*, one observes with a sigh),
But in Algebra—*there* she's unique,
  But her forte's to evaluate π.

She can talk about putting a "spirt on"
  (I admit, an unmaidenly freak),
And she dearly delighteth to flirt on
  A punt in some shadowy creek;
Should her bark, by mischance, spring a leak,
  She can swim as a swallow can fly;
She can fence, she can put with a cleek,
  But her forte's to evaluate π.

She has lectured on Scopas and Myrton,
  Coins, vases, mosaics, the antique,
Old tiles with the secular dirt on,
  Old marbles with noses to seek.
And her Cobet she quotes by the week,
  And she's written on κεν and on καὶ,
And her service is swift and oblique,
  But her forte's to evaluate π.

ENVOY.

Princess, like a rose is her cheek,
  And her eyes are as blue as the sky,
And I'd speak, had I courage to speak,
  But—her forte's to evaluate π.

RONSARD'S GRAVE.

YE wells, ye founts that fall
  From the steep mountain wall,
That fall, and flash, and fleet
    With silver feet,

Ye woods, ye streams that lave
The meadows with your wave,

>   Ye hills, and valley fair,
>   Attend my prayer!
>
> When Heaven and Fate decree
> My latest hour for me,
>   When I must pass away
>   From pleasant day,
>
> I ask that none may break
> The marble for my sake,
>   Wishful to make more fair
>   My sepulchre.
>
> Only a laurel tree
> Shall shade the grave of me,
>   Only Apollo's bough
>   Shall guard me now!
>
> Now shall I be at rest
> Among the spirits blest,
>   The happy dead that dwell—
>   Where,—who may tell?
>
> The snow and wind and hail
> May never there prevail,
>   Nor ever thunder fall
>   Nor storm at all.
>
> But always fadeless there
> The woods are green and fair,
>   And faithful ever more
>   Spring to that shore!
>
> There shall I ever hear
> Alcaeus' music clear,
>   And sweetest of all things
>   There SAPPHO sings.

SAN TERENZO.

(The village in the bay of Spezia, near which Shelley was living before the wreck of the *Don Juan*.)

> MID April seemed like some November day,
>   When through the glassy waters, dull as lead
> Our boat, like shadowy barques that bear the dead,
>   Slipped down the long shores of the Spezian bay,
>   Rounded a point,—and San Terenzo lay

Before us, that gay village, yellow and red,
The roof that covered Shelley's homeless head,—
   His house, a place deserted, bleak and grey.

The waves broke on the door-step; fishermen
   Cast their long nets, and drew, and cast again.
   Deep in the ilex woods we wandered free,
When suddenly the forest glades were stirred
   With waving pinions, and a great sea bird
Flew forth, like Shelley's spirit, to the sea!

1880.

ROMANCE.

My Love dwelt in a Northern land.
   A grey tower in a forest green
Was hers, and far on either hand
   The long wash of the waves was seen,
And leagues on leagues of yellow sand,
   The woven forest boughs between!

And through the silver Northern night
   The sunset slowly died away,
And herds of strange deer, lily-white,
   Stole forth among the branches grey;
About the coming of the light,
   They fled like ghosts before the day!

I know not if the forest green
   Still girdles round that castle grey;
I know not if the boughs between
   The white deer vanish ere the day;
Above my Love the grass is green,
   My heart is colder than the clay!

BALLADE OF HIS OWN COUNTRY.

I scribbled on a fly-book's leaves
   Among the shining salmon-flies;
A song for summer-time that grieves
   I scribbled on a fly-book's leaves.
   Between grey sea and golden sheaves,
Beneath the soft wet Morvern skies,
I scribbled on a fly-book's leaves
   Among the shining salmon-flies.

TO C. H. ARKCOLL.

LET them boast of Arabia, oppressed
   By the odour of myrrh on the breeze;
In the isles of the East and the West
   That are sweet with the cinnamon trees
Let the sandal-wood perfume the seas
   Give the roses to Rhodes and to Crete,
We are more than content, if you please,
   With the smell of bog-myrtle and peat!

Though Dan Virgil enjoyed himself best
   With the scent of the limes, when the bees
Hummed low 'round the doves in their nest,
   While the vintagers lay at their ease,
Had he sung in our northern degrees,
   He'd have sought a securer retreat,
He'd have dwelt, where the heart of us flees,
   With the smell of bog-myrtle and peat!

Oh, the broom has a chivalrous crest
   And the daffodil's fair on the leas,
And the soul of the Southron might rest,
   And be perfectly happy with these;
But *we*, that were nursed on the knees
   Of the hills of the North, we would fleet
Where our hearts might their longing appease
   With the smell of bog-myrtle and peat!

ENVOY.

   Ah Constance, the land of our quest
      It is far from the sounds of the street,
   Where the Kingdom of Galloway's blest
      With the smell of bog-myrtle and peat!

VILLANELLE.

(TO M. JOSEPH BOULMIER, AUTHOR OF "LES VILLANELLES.")

   VILLANELLE, why art thou mute?
      Hath the singer ceased to sing?
   Hath the Master lost his lute?

   Many a pipe and scrannel flute
      On the breeze their discords fling;
   Villanelle, why art *thou* mute?

Sound of tumult and dispute,
Noise of war the echoes bring;
Hath the Master lost his lute?

Once he sang of bud and shoot
  In the season of the Spring;
Villanelle, why art thou mute?

Fading leaf and falling fruit
  Say, "The year is on the wing,
Hath the Master lost his lute?"

Ere the axe lie at the root,
  Ere the winter come as king,
Villanelle, why art thou mute?
Hath the Master lost his lute?

TRIOLETS AFTER MOSCHUS.

Αἰαῖ ταὶ μαλάχαι μὲν ἐπὰν κατὰ κᾶπον ὄλωντα
ὕστερον αὖ ζώοντι καὶ εἰς ἔτος ἄλλο φύοντι
ἄμμες δ' οἱ μεγάλοι καὶ καρτεροί, οἱ σοφοὶ ἄνδες
ὁππότε πρᾶτα θάνωμες, ἀνάκοοι ἐν χθονὶ κοίλᾳ,
εὕδομες εὖ μάλα μακρὸν ἀτέρμονα νήγρετον ὕπνον.

ALAS, for us no second spring,
  Like mallows in the garden-bed,
For these the grave has lost his sting,
  Alas, for *us* no second spring,
  Who sleep without awakening,
And, dead, for ever more are dead,
  Alas, for us no second spring,
    Like mallows in the garden-bed!

Alas, the strong, the wise, the brave,
  That boast themselves the sons of men!
Once they go down into the grave—
  Alas, the strong, the wise, the brave,—
  They perish and have none to save,
  They are sown, and are not raised again;
Alas, the strong, the wise, the brave,
  That boast themselves the sons of men!

BALLADE OF CRICKET.

TO T. W. LANG.

THE burden of hard hitting: slog away!
Here shalt thou make a "five" and there a "four,"
And then upon thy bat shalt lean, and say,
That thou art in for an uncommon score.
Yea, the loud ring applauding thee shall roar,
And thou to rival THORNTON shalt aspire,
When lo, the Umpire gives thee "leg before,"—
"This is the end of every man's desire!"

The burden of much bowling, when the stay
Of all thy team is "collared," swift or slower,
When "bailers" break not in their wonted way,
And "yorkers" come not off as here-to-fore,
When length balls shoot no more, ah never more,
When all deliveries lose their former fire,
When bats seem broader than the broad barn-door,—
"This is the end of every man's desire!"

The burden of long fielding, when the clay
Clings to thy shoon in sudden shower's downpour,
And running still thou stumblest, or the ray
Of blazing suns doth bite and burn thee sore,
And blind thee till, forgetful of thy lore,
Thou dost most mournfully misjudge a "skyer,"
And lose a match the Fates cannot restore,—
"This is the end of every man's desire!"

ENVOY.

Alas, yet liefer on Youth's hither shore
Would I be some poor Player on scant hire,
Than King among the old, who play no more,—
"*This* is the end of every man's desire!"

THE LAST MAYING.

"It is told of the last Lovers which watched May-night in the
forest, before men brought the tidings of the Gospel to this land, that
they beheld no Fairies, nor Dwarfs, nor no such Thing, but the very
Venus herself, who bade them 'make such cheer as they

might,
　　for' said she, 'I shall live no more in these Woods, nor shall ye
　　endure to see another May time.'"—EDMUND GORLIOT,
　　"Of Phantasies and Omens," . (1573.)

"WHENCE do ye come, with the dew on your hair?
From what far land are the boughs ye bear,
　　The blossoms and buds upon breasts and tresses,
The light burned white in your faces fair?"

"In a falling fane have we built our house,
With the dying Gods we have held carouse,
　　And our lips are wan from their wild caresses,
Our hands are filled with their holy boughs.

As we crossed the lawn in the dying day
No fairy led us to meet the May,
　　But the very Goddess loved by lovers,
In mourning raiment of green and grey.

She was not decked as for glee and game,
She was not veiled with the veil of flame,
　　The saffron veil of the Bride that covers
The face that is flushed with her joy and shame.

On the laden branches the scent and dew
Mingled and met, and as snow to strew
　　The woodland rides and the fragrant grasses,
White flowers fell as the night wind blew.

Tears and kisses on lips and eyes
Mingled and met amid laughter and sighs
　　For grief that abides, and joy that passes,
For pain that tarries and mirth that flies.

It chanced as the dawning grew to grey
Pale and sad on our homeward way,
　　With weary lips, and palled with pleasure
The Goddess met us, farewell to say.

"Ye have made your choice, and the better part,
Ye chose" she said, "and the wiser art;
　　In the wild May night drank all the measure,
The perfect pleasure of heart and heart.

"Ye shall walk no more with the May," she said,
"Shall your love endure though the Gods be dead?

Shall the flitting flocks, mine own, my chosen,
Sing as of old, and be happy and wed?

"Yea, they are glad as of old; but you,
Fair and fleet as the dawn or the dew,
   Abide no more, for the springs are frozen,
And fled the Gods that ye loved and knew.

"Ye shall never know Summer again like this;
Ye shall play no more with the Fauns, I wis,
   No more in the nymphs' and dryads' playtime
Shall echo and answer kiss and kiss.

"Though the flowers in your golden hair be bright,
Your golden hair shall be waste and white
   On faded brows ere another May time
      Bring the spring, but no more delight."

HOMERIC UNITY.

THE sacred keep of Ilion is rent
   By shaft and pit; foiled waters wander slow
Through plains where Simois and Scamander went
   To war with Gods and heroes long ago.
   Not yet to tired Cassandra, lying low
In rich Mycenæ, do the Fates relent:
   The bones of Agamemnon are a show,
And ruined is his royal monument.

The dust and awful treasures of the Dead,
   Hath Learning scattered wide, but vainly thee,
Homer, she meteth with her tool of lead,
   And strives to rend thy songs; too blind to see
The crown that burns on thine immortal head
   Of indivisible supremacy!

IN TINTAGEL.

LUI.

   AH lady, lady, leave the creeping mist,
      And leave the iron castle by the sea!

ELLE.

   Nay, from the sea there came a ghost that kissed
      My lips, and so I cannot come to thee!

LUI.

>Ah lady, leave the cruel landward wind
>   That crusts the blighted flowers with bitter foam!

ELLE.

>Nay, for his arms are cold and strong to bind,
>   And I must dwell with him and make my home!

LUI.

>Come, for the Spring is fair in Joyous Guard
>   And down deep alleys sweet birds sing again.

ELLE.

>But I must tarry with the winter hard,
>   And with the bitter memory of pain,
>Although the Spring be fair in Joyous Guard,
>   And in the gardens glad birds sing again!

PISIDICÊ.

The incident is from the Love Stories of Parthenius, who preserved fragments of a lost epic on the expedition of Achilles against Lesbos, an island allied with Troy.

>THE daughter of the Lesbian king
>   Within her bower she watched the war,
>Far off she heard the arrows ring,
>   The smitten harness ring afar;
>And, fighting from the foremost car,
>   Saw one that smote where all must flee;
>More fair than the Immortals are
>   He seemed to fair Pisidicê!

>She saw, she loved him, and her heart
>   Before Achilles, Peleus' son,
>Threw all its guarded gates apart,
>   A maiden fortress lightly won!
>And, ere that day of fight was done,
>   No more of land or faith recked she,
>But joyed in her new life begun,—
>   Her life of love, Pisidicê!

>She took a gift into her hand,
>   As one that had a boon to crave;
>She stole across the ruined land
>   Where lay the dead without a grave,
>And to Achilles' hand she gave

    Her gift, the secret postern's key.
"To-morrow let me be thy slave!"
    Moaned to her love Pisidicê.

Ere dawn the Argives' clarion call
    Rang down Methymna's burning street;
They slew the sleeping warriors all,
    They drove the women to the fleet,
Save one, that to Achilles' feet
    Clung, but, in sudden wrath, cried he:
"For her no doom but death is meet,"
    And there men stoned Pisidicê.

In havens of that haunted coast,
    Amid the myrtles of the shore,
The moon sees many a maiden ghost
    Love's outcast now and evermore.
The silence hears the shades deplore
    Their hour of dear-bought love; but *thee*
The waves lull, 'neath thine olives hoar,
    To dreamless rest, Pisidicê!

FROM THE EAST TO THE WEST.

RETURNING from what other seas
    Dost thou renew thy murmuring,
Weak Tide, and hast thou aught of these
    To tell, the shores where float and cling
My love, my hope, my memories?

Say does my lady wake to note
    The gold light into silver die?
Or do thy waves make lullaby,
    While dreams of hers, like angels, float
Through star-sown spaces of the sky?

Ah, would such angels came to me
    That dreams of mine might speak with hers,
Nor wake the slumber of the sea
    With words as low as winds that be
Awake among the gossamers!

LOVE THE VAMPIRE.

Ο ΕΡΩΤΑΣ 'Σ ΤΟΝ ΤΑΦΟ.

    THE level sands and grey,
    Stretch leagues and leagues away,

Down to the border line of sky and foam,
   A spark of sunset burns,
   The grey tide-water turns,
Back, like a ghost from her forbidden home!

   Here, without pyre or bier,
   Light Love was buried here,
Alas, his grave was wide and deep enough,
   Thrice, with averted head,
   We cast dust on the dead,
And left him to his rest. An end of Love.

   "No stone to roll away,
   No seal of snow or clay,
Only soft dust above his wearied eyes,
   But though the sudden sound
   Of Doom should shake the ground,
And graves give up their ghosts, he will not rise!"

   So each to each we said!
   Ah, but to either bed
Set far apart in lands of North and South,
   Love as a Vampire came
   With haggard eyes aflame,
And kissed us with the kisses of his mouth!

   Thenceforth in dreams must we
   Each other's shadow see
Wand'ring unsatisfied in empty lands,
   Still the desirèd face
   Fleets from the vain embrace,
And still the shape evades the longing hands.

BALLADE OF THE BOOK-MAN'S PARADISE

THERE *is* a Heaven, or here, or there,—
A Heaven there is, for me and you,
Where bargains meet for purses spare,
Like ours, are not so far and few.
Thuanus' bees go humming through
The learned groves, 'neath rainless skies,
O'er volumes old and volumes new,
Within that Book-man's Paradise!

There treasures bound for Longepierre
Keep brilliant their morocco blue,
There Hookes' *Amanda* is not rare,

Nor early tracts upon Peru!
Racine is common as Rotrou,
No Shakespeare Quarto search defies,
And Caxtons grow as blossoms grew,
Within that Book-man's Paradise!

There's Eve,—not our first mother fair,—
But Clovis Eve, a binder true;
Thither does Bauzonnet repair,
Derome, Le Gascon, Padeloup!
But never come the cropping crew
That dock a volume's honest size,
Nor they that "letter" backs askew,
Within that Book-man's Paradise!

ENVOY.

Friend, do not Heber and De Thou,
And Scott, and Southey, kind and wise,
La chasse au bouquin still pursue
Within that Book-man's Paradise?

BALLADE OF A FRIAR.

(Clement Marot's *Frère Lubin*, though translated by Longfellow and others, has not hitherto been rendered into the original measure of *ballade à double refrain*.)

SOME ten or twenty times a day,
To bustle to the town with speed,
To dabble in what dirt he may,—
Le Frère Lubin's the man you need!
But any sober life to lead
Upon an exemplary plan,
Requires a Christian indeed,—
Le Frère Lubin is *not* the man!

Another's wealth on his to lay,
With all the craft of guile and greed,
To leave you bare of pence or pay,—
Le Frère Lubin's the man you need!
But watch him with the closest heed,
And dun him with what force you can,—
He'll not refund, howe'er you plead,—
Le Frère Lubin is *not* the man!

An honest girl to lead astray,
With subtle saw and promised meed,
Requires no cunning crone and grey,—
Le Frère Lubin's the man you need!
He preaches an ascetic creed,
But,—try him with the water can—
A dog will drink, whate'er his breed,—
Le Frère Lubin is *not* the man!

ENVOY.

In good to fail, in ill succeed,
Le Frère Lubin's the man you need!
In honest works to lead the van,
Le Frère Lubin is *not* the man!

BALLADE OF NEGLECTED MERIT. [194]

I HAVE scribbled in verse and in prose,
I have painted "arrangements in greens,"
And my name is familiar to those
Who take in the high class magazines;
I compose; I've invented machines;
I have written an "Essay on Rhyme";
For my county I played, in my teens,
But—I am not in "Men of the Time!"

I have lived, as a chief, with the Crows;
I have "interviewed" Princes and Queens;
I have climbed the Caucasian snows;
I abstain, like the ancients, from beans,—
I've a guess what Pythagoras means
When he says that to eat them's a crime,—
I have lectured upon the Essenes,
But—I am not in "Men of the Time!"

I've a fancy as morbid as Poe's,
I can tell what is meant by "Shebeens,"
I have breasted the river that flows
Through the land of the wild Gadarenes;
I can gossip with Burton on *skenes*,
I can imitate Irving (the Mime),
And my sketches are quainter than Keene's,
But—I am not in "Men of the Time!"

ENVOY.

So the tower of mine eminence leans
Like the Pisan, and mud is its lime;
I'm acquainted with Dukes and with Deans,
But—I am not in "Men of the Time!"

BALLADE OF RAILWAY NOVELS.

LET others praise analysis
  And revel in a "cultured" style,
And follow the subjective Miss [196]
  From Boston to the banks of Nile,
Rejoice in anti-British bile,
  And weep for fickle hero's woe,
These twain have shortened many a mile,
  Miss Braddon and Gaboriau.

These damsels of "Democracy's,"
  How long they stop at every stile!
They smile, and we are told, I wis,
  Ten subtle reasons *why* they smile.
Give *me* your villains deeply vile,
  Give me Lecoq, Jottrat, and Co.,
Great artists of the ruse and wile,
  Miss Braddon and Gaboriau!

Oh, novel readers, tell me this,
  Can prose that's polished by the file,
Like great Boisgobey's mysteries,
  Wet days and weary ways beguile,
And man to living reconcile,
  Like these whose every trick we know?
The agony how high they pile,
  Miss Braddon and Gaboriau!

ENVOY.

  Ah, friend, how many and many a while
    They've made the slow time fleetly flow,
  And solaced pain and charmed exile,
    Miss Braddon and Gaboriau.

THE CLOUD CHORUS.

(FROM ARISTOPHANES.)

Socrates speaks.

HITHER, come hither, ye Clouds renowned, and unveil yourselves here;
Come, though ye dwell on the sacred crests of Olympian snow,
Or whether ye dance with the Nereid choir in the gardens clear,
Or whether your golden urns are dipped in Nile's overflow,
Or whether you dwell by Mæotis mere
Or the snows of Mimas, arise! appear!
And hearken to us, and accept our gifts ere ye rise and go.

The Clouds sing.

Immortal Clouds from the echoing shore
Of the father of streams, from the sounding sea,
Dewy and fleet, let us rise and soar.
Dewy and gleaming, and fleet are we!
Let us look on the tree-clad mountain crest,
   On the sacred earth where the fruits rejoice,
On the waters that murmur east and west
   On the tumbling sea with his moaning voice,
For unwearied glitters the Eye of the Air,
   And the bright rays gleam;
Then cast we our shadows of mist, and fare
In our deathless shapes to glance everywhere
   From the height of the heaven, on the land and air,
     And the Ocean stream.

Let us on, ye Maidens that bring the Rain,
   Let us gaze on Pallas' citadel,
    In the country of Cecrops, fair and dear
    The mystic land of the holy cell,
   Where the Rites unspoken securely dwell,
   And the gifts of the Gods that know not stain
And a people of mortals that know not fear.
For the temples tall, and the statues fair,
And the feasts of the Gods are holiest there,
The feasts of Immortals, the chaplets of flowers
   And the Bromian mirth at the coming of spring,
And the musical voices that fill the hours,
   And the dancing feet of the Maids that sing!

BALLADE OF LITERARY FAME.

"All these for Fourpence."

OH, where are the endless Romances
Our grandmothers used to adore?
The Knights with their helms and their lances,

Their shields and the favours they wore?
And the Monks with their magical lore?
They have passed to Oblivion and *Nox*,
They have fled to the shadowy shore,—
They are all in the Fourpenny Box!

And where the poetical fancies
Our fathers rejoiced in, of yore?
The lyric's melodious expanses,
The Epics in cantos a score?
They have been and are not: no more
Shall the shepherds drive silvery flocks,
Nor the ladies their languors deplore,—
They are all in the Fourpenny Box!

And the Music! The songs and the dances?
The tunes that Time may not restore?
And the tomes where Divinity prances?
And the pamphlets where Heretics roar?
They have ceased to be even a bore,—
The Divine, and the Sceptic who mocks,—
They are "cropped," they are "foxed" to the core,—
They are all in the Fourpenny Box!

ENVOY.

Suns beat on them; tempests downpour,
On the chest without cover or locks,
Where they lie by the Bookseller's door,—
They are *all* in the Fourpenny Box!

Νήνεμος Αἰών.

I WOULD my days had been in other times,
A moment in the long unnumbered years
That knew the sway of Horus and of hawk,
In peaceful lands that border on the Nile.

I would my days had been in other times,
Lulled by the sacrifice and mumbled hymn
Between the Five great Rivers, or in shade
And shelter of the cool Himâlayan hills.

I would my days had been in other times,
That I in some old abbey of Touraine
Had watched the rounding grapes, and lived my life,
Ere ever Luther came or Rabelais!

I would my days had been in other times,
When quiet life to death not terrible
Drifted, as ashes of the Santhal dead
Drift down the sacred Rivers to the Sea!

SCIENCE.

THE BARBAROUS BIRD-GODS: A SAVAGE PARABASIS.

In the *Aves* of Aristophanes, the Bird Chorus declare that they are older than the Gods, and greater benefactors of men. This idea recurs in almost all savage mythologies, and I have made the savage Bird-gods state their own case.

The Birds sing.

> WE would have you to wit, that on eggs though we sit, and are spiked on the spit, and are baked in the pan,
> Birds are older by far than your ancestors are, and made love and made war ere the making of Man!
> For when all things were dark, not a glimmer nor spark, and the world like a barque without rudder or sail
> Floated on through the night, 'twas a Bird struck a light, 'twas a flash from the bright feather'd Tonatiu's [207] tail!
> Then the Hawk [208a] with some dry wood flew up in the sky, and afar, safe and high, the Hawk lit Sun and Moon,
> And the Birds of the air they rejoiced everywhere, and they recked not of care that should come on them soon.
> For the Hawk, so they tell, was then known as Pundjel, [208b] and a-musing he fell at the close of the day;
> Then he went on the quest, as we thought, of a nest, with some bark of the best, and a clawful of clay. [208c]
> And with these did he frame two birds lacking a name, without feathers (his game was a puzzle to all);
> Next around them he fluttered a-dancing, and muttered; and, lastly, he uttered a magical call:
> Then the figures of clay, as they featherless lay, they leaped up, who but they, and embracing they fell,
> And *this* was the baking of Man, and his making; but now he's forsaking his Father, Pundjel!
> Now these creatures of mire, they kept whining for fire, and to crown their desire who was found but the Wren?
> To the high heaven he came, from the Sun stole he flame, and for this has a name in the memory of men! [209a]
> And in India who for the Soma juice flew, and to men brought it through without falter or fail?

Why the Hawk 'twas again, and great Indra to men would appear, now and then, in the shape of a Quail,
While the Thlinkeet's delight is the Bird of the Night, the beak and the bright ebon plumage of Yehl. [209b]
And who for man's need brought the famed Suttung's mead? why 'tis told in the creed of the Sagamen strong,
'Twas the Eagle god who brought the drink from the blue, and gave mortals the brew that's the fountain of song. [210a]
Next, who gave men their laws? and what reason or cause the young brave overawes when in need of a squaw,
Till he thinks it a shame to wed one of his name, and his conduct you blame if he thus breaks the law?
For you still hold it wrong if a *lubra* [210b] belong to the self-same *kobong* [210c] that is Father of you,
To take *her* as a bride to your ebony side; nay, you give her a wide berth; quite right of you, too.
For *her* father, you know, is *your* father, the Crow, and no blessing but woe from the wedding would spring.
Well, these rules they were made in the wattle-gum shade, and were strictly obeyed, when the Crow was the King. [210d]
Thus on Earth's little ball to the Birds you owe all, yet your gratitude's small for the favours they've done,
And their feathers you pill, and you eat them at will, yes, you plunder and kill the bright birds one by one;
There's a price on their head, and the Dodo is dead, and the Moa has fled from the sight of the sun!

MAN AND THE ASCIDIAN.

A MORALITY.

"THE Ancestor remote of Man,"
Says Darwin, "is th' Ascidian,"
A scanty sort of water-beast
That, ninety million years at least
Before Gorillas came to be,
Went swimming up and down the sea.

Their ancestors the pious praise,
And like to imitate their ways;
How, then, does our first parent live,
What lesson has his life to give?

Th' Ascidian tadpole, young and gay,
Doth Life with one bright eye survey,
His consciousness has easy play.

He's sensitive to grief and pain,
Has tail, and spine, and bears a brain,
And everything that fits the state
Of creatures we call vertebrate.
But age comes on; with sudden shock
He sticks his head against a rock!
His tail drops off, his eye drops in,
His brain's absorbed into his skin;
He does not move, nor feel, nor know
The tidal water's ebb and flow,
But still abides, unstirred, alone,
A sucker sticking to a stone.

And we, his children, truly we
In youth are, like the Tadpole, free.
And where we would we blithely go,
Have brains and hearts, and feel and know.
Then Age comes on! To Habit we
Affix ourselves and are not free;
Th' Ascidian's rooted to a rock,
And we are bond-slaves of the clock;
Our rocks are Medicine—Letters—Law,
From these our heads we cannot draw:
Our loves drop off, our hearts drop in,
And daily thicker grows our skin.

Ah, scarce we live, we scarcely know
The wide world's moving ebb and flow,
The clanging currents ring and shock,
But we are rooted to the rock.
And thus at ending of his span,
Blind, deaf, and indolent, does Man
Revert to the Ascidian.

BALLADE OF THE PRIMITIVE JEST.

> "What did the dark-haired Iberian laugh at before the tall blonde
> Aryan drove him into the corners of Europe?"—*Brander Matthews.*

I AM an ancient Jest!
Palæolithic man
In his arboreal nest
The sparks of fun would fan;
My outline did he plan,

And laughed like one possessed,
'Twas thus my course began,
I am a Merry Jest!

I am an early Jest!
Man delved, and built, and span;
Then wandered South and West
The peoples Aryan,
I journeyed in their van;
The Semites, too, confessed,—
From Beersheba to Dan,—
I am a Merry Jest!

I am an ancient Jest,
Through all the human clan,
Red, black, white, free, oppressed,
Hilarious I ran!
I'm found in Lucian,
In Poggio, and the rest,
I'm dear to Moll and Nan!
I am a Merry Jest!

ENVOY.

Prince, you may storm and ban—
Joe Millers *are* a pest,
Suppress me if you can!
I am a Merry Jest!

CAMEOS.
SONNETS FROM THE ANTIQUE.

These versions from classical passages are pretty close to the original, except where compression was needed, as in the sonnets from Pausanias and Apuleius, or where, as in the case of fragments of Æschylus and Sophocles, a little expansion was required.

CAMEOS.

THE graver by Apollo's shrine,
  Before the Gods had fled, would stand,
  A shell or onyx in his hand,
To copy there the face divine,
Till earnest touches, line by line,
  Had wrought the wonder of the land
  Within a beryl's golden band,
Or on some fiery opal fine.

Ah! would that as some ancient ring
To us, on shell or stone, doth bring,
   Art's marvels perished long ago,
So I, within the sonnet's space,
   The large Hellenic lines might trace,
     The statue in the cameo!

HELEN ON THE WALLS.

(*Iliad*, iii. 146.)

FAIR Helen to the Scæan portals came,
Where sat the elders, peers of Priamus,
Thymoetas, Hiketaon, Panthöus,
And many another of a noble name,
Famed warriors, now in council more of fame.
Always above the gates, in converse thus
They chattered like cicalas garrulous;
Who marking Helen, swore "it is no shame
That armed Achæan knights, and Ilian men
For such a woman's sake should suffer long.
Fair as a deathless goddess seemeth she.
Nay, but aboard the red-prowed ships again
Home let her pass in peace, not working wrong
To us, and children's children yet to be."

THE ISLES OF THE BLESSED.

Pindar, Fr., 106, 107 (95): B. 4, 129–130, 109 (97): B. 4, 132.

NOW the light of the sun, in the night of the Earth, on the souls of the True
   Shines, and their city is girt with the meadow where reigneth the rose;
And deep is the shade of the woods, and the wind that flits o'er them and through
   Sings of the sea, and is sweet from the isles where the frankincense blows:
Green is their garden and orchard, with rare fruits golden it glows,
   And the souls of the Blessed are glad in the pleasures on Earth that they knew,
And in chariots these have delight, and in dice and in minstrelsy those,
   And the savour of sacrifice clings to the altars and rises anew.

But the Souls that Persephone cleanses from ancient pollution and stain,
   These at the end of the age, be they prince, be they singer, or seer;
These to the world shall be born as of old, shall be sages again;

These of their hands shall be hardy, shall live, and shall die, and shall hear
Thanks of the people, and songs of the minstrels that praise them amain,
   And their glory shall dwell in the land where they dwelt, while year calls unto year!

DEATH.

(*Æsch., Fr.*, 156.)

  OF all Gods Death alone
    Disdaineth sacrifice:
  No man hath found or shown
    The gift that Death would prize.
    In vain are songs or sighs,
  Pæan, or praise, or moan,
    Alone beneath the skies
  Hath Death no altar-stone!

  There is no head so dear
    That men would grudge to Death;
  Let Death but ask, we give
  All gifts that we may live;
  But though Death dwells so near,
    We know not what he saith.

NYSA.

(*Soph., Fr.*, 235; *Æsch., Fr.*, 56.)

  ON these Nysæan shores divine
    The clusters ripen in a day.
    At dawn the blossom shreds away;
  The berried grapes are green and fine
  And full by noon; in day's decline
    They're purple with a bloom of grey,
    And e'er the twilight plucked are they,
  And crushed, by nightfall, into wine.

  But through the night with torch in hand
    Down the dusk hills the Mænads fare;
    The bull-voiced mummers roar and blare,
  The muffled timbrels swell and sound,
    And drown the clamour of the band
  Like thunder moaning underground.

COLONUS.

(*Œd. Col.*, 667–705.)

I.

    HERE be the fairest homes the land can show,
        The silvery-cliffed Colonus; always here
    The nightingale doth haunt and singeth clear,
    For well the deep green gardens doth she know.
    Groves of the God, where winds may never blow,
        Nor men may tread, nor noontide sun may peer
        Among the myriad-berried ivy dear,
    Where Dionysus wanders to and fro.

    For here he loves to dwell, and here resort
    These Nymphs that are his nurses and his court,
    And golden eyed beneath the dewy boughs
        The crocus burns, and the narcissus fair
        Clusters his blooms to crown thy clustered hair,
    Demeter, and to wreathe the Maiden's brows!

II.

    YEA, here the dew of Heaven upon the grain
        Fails never, nor the ceaseless water-spring,
        Near neighbour of Cephisus wandering,
    That day by day revisiteth the plain.
    Nor do the Goddesses the grove disdain,
        But chiefly here the Muses quire and sing,
        And here they love to weave their dancing ring,
    With Aphrodite of the golden rein.

    And here there springs a plant that knoweth not
        The Asian mead, nor that great Dorian isle,
    Unsown, untilled, within our garden plot
        It dwells, the grey-leaved olive; ne'er shall guile
    Nor force of foemen root it from the spot:
        Zeus and Athene guarding it the while!

THE PASSING OF ŒDIPOUS.

(*Œd. Col.*, 1655–1666.)

    HOW Œdipous departed, who may tell
        Save Theseus only? for there neither came
        The burning bolt of thunder, and the flame
    To blast him into nothing, nor the swell
    Of sea-tide spurred by tempest on him fell.
        But some diviner herald none may name

    Called him, or inmost Earth's abyss became
    The painless place where such a soul might dwell.

    Howe'er it chanced, untouched of malady,
      Unharmed by fear, unfollowed by lament,
    With comfort on the twilight way he went,
      Passing, if ever man did, wondrously;
    From this world's death to life divinely rent,
      Unschooled in Time's last lesson, how we die.

THE TAMING OF TYRO.

(*Soph.*, *Fr.*, 587.)

(Sidero, the stepmother of Tyro, daughter of Salmoneus, cruelly entreated her in all things, and chiefly in this, that she let sheer her beautiful hair.)

    AT fierce Sidero's word the thralls drew near,
      And shore the locks of Tyro,—like ripe corn
        They fell in golden harvest,—but forlorn
    The maiden shuddered in her pain and fear,
      Like some wild mare that cruel grooms in scorn
    Hunt in the meadows, and her mane they sheer,
    And drive her where, within the waters clear,
      She spies her shadow, and her shame doth mourn.

    Ah! hard were he and pitiless of heart
      Who marking that wild thing made weak and tame,
        Broken, and grieving for her glory gone,
    Could mock her grief; but scornfully apart
      Sidero stood, and watched a wind that came
    And tossed the curls like fire that flew and shone!

TO ARTEMIS.

(*Hippol.*, *Eurip.*, 73–87.)

    FOR thee soft crowns in thine untrampled mead
      I wove, my lady, and to thee I bear;
    Thither no shepherd drives his flocks to feed,
      Nor scythe of steel has ever laboured there;
      Nay, through the spring among the blossoms fair
    The brown bee comes and goes, and with good heed
    Thy maiden, Reverence, sweet streams doth lead
      About the grassy close that is her care!

    Souls only that are gracious and serene
      By gift of God, in human lore unread,

    May pluck these holy blooms and grasses green
        That now I wreathe for thine immortal head,
    I that may walk with thee, thyself unseen,
        And by thy whispered voice am comforted.

CRITICISM OF LIFE.

(*Hippol.*, *Eurip.*, 252–266.)

    LONG life hath taught me many things, and shown
        That lukewarm loves for men who die are best,
        Weak wine of liking let them mix alone,
    Not Love, that stings the soul within the breast;
    Happy, who wears his love-bonds lightliest,
        Now cherished, now away at random thrown!
        Grievous it is for other's grief to moan,
    Hard that my soul for thine should lose her rest!

    Wise ruling this of life: but yet again
        Perchance too rigid diet is not well;
    He lives not best who dreads the coming pain
        And shunneth each delight desirable:
    Flee thou extremes, this word alone is plain,
        Of all that God hath given to Man to spell!

AMARYLLIS.

(Theocritus, Idyll, iii.)

    FAIR Amaryllis, wilt thou never peep
        From forth the cave, and call me, and be mine?
    Lo, apples ten I bear thee from the steep,
        These didst thou long for, and all these are thine.
    Ah, would I were a honey-bee to sweep
        Through ivy, and the bracken, and woodbine;
    To watch thee waken, Love, and watch thee sleep,
        Within thy grot below the shadowy pine.
    Now know I Love, a cruel god is he,
        The wild beast bare him in the wild wood drear;
    And truly to the bone he burneth me.
        But, black-browed Amaryllis, ne'er a tear,
    Nor sigh, nor blush, nor aught have I from thee;
        Nay, nor a kiss, a little gift and dear.

THE CANNIBAL ZEUS.

A.D. 160.

> Καὶ ἔθυσε τὸ βρέφος, καὶ ἔσπεισεν ἐπὶ τοῦ βωμοῦ τὸ
> αἷμα—ἐπὶ τούτου βωμοῦ τῷ Δὺ θύουσιν ἐν ἀποῤῥήτῳ.—
> *Paus.* viii. 38.

NONE elder city doth the Sun behold
   Than ancient Lycosura; 'twas begun
   Ere Zeus the meat of mortals learned to shun,
And here hath he a grove whose haunted fold
The driven deer seek and huntsmen dread: 'tis told
   That whoso fares within that forest dun
   Thenceforth shall cast no shadow in the Sun,
Ay, and within the year his life is cold!

Hard by dwelt he [232] who, while the Gods deigned eat
At good men's tables, gave them dreadful meat,
   A child he slew:—his mountain altar green
Here still hath Zeus, with rites untold of me,
Piteous, but as they are let these things be,
   And as from the beginning they have been!

INVOCATION OF ISIS.

(*Apuleius*, Metamorph. XI.)

THOU that art sandalled on immortal feet
   With leaves of palm, the prize of Victory;
Thou that art crowned with snakes and blossoms sweet,
   Queen of the silver dews and shadowy sky,
   I pray thee by all names men name thee by!
Demeter, come, and leave the yellow wheat!
   Or Aphrodite, let thy lovers sigh!
Or Dian, from thine Asian temple fleet!

Or, yet more dread, divine Persephone
   From worlds of wailing spectres, ah, draw near;
Approach, Selene, from thy subject sea;
   Come, Artemis, and this night spare the deer:
By all thy names and rites I summon thee;
   By all thy rites and names, Our Lady, hear!

THE COMING OF ISIS.

SO Lucius prayed, and sudden, from afar,
   Floated the locks of Isis, shone the bright
Crown that is tressed with berry, snake, and star;
   She came in deep blue raiment of the night,
   Above her robes that now were snowy white,

Now golden as the moons of harvest are,
Now red, now flecked with many a cloudy bar,
   Now stained with all the lustre of the light.

Then he who saw her knew her, and he knew
   The awful symbols borne in either hand;
The golden urn that laves Demeter's dew,
   The handles wreathed with asps, the mystic wand;
The shaken seistron's music, tinkling through
   The temples of that old Osirian land.

THE SPINET.

MY heart's an old Spinet with strings
   To laughter chiefly tuned, but some
   That Fate has practised hard on, dumb,
They answer not whoever sings.
The ghosts of half-forgotten things
   Will touch the keys with fingers numb,
   The little mocking spirits come
And thrill it with their fairy wings.

A jingling harmony it makes
   My heart, my lyre, my old Spinet,
And now a memory it wakes,
   And now the music means "forget,"
And little heed the player takes
   Howe'er the thoughtful critic fret.

NOTES.

Page 127. *The Fortunate Islands.* This piece is a rhymed loose version of a passage in the *Vera Historia* of Lucian. The humorist was unable to resist the temptation to introduce passages of mockery, which are here omitted. Part of his description of the Isles of the Blest has a close and singular resemblance to the New Jerusalem of the Apocalypse. The clear River of Life and the prodigality of gold and of precious stones may especially be noticed.

Page 133. *Whoso doth taste the Dead Men's bread, &c.* This belief that the living may visit, on occasion, the dwellings of the dead, but can never return to earth if they taste the food of the departed, is expressed in myths of worldwide distribution. Because she ate the pomegranate seed, Persephone became subject to the spell of Hades. In Apuleius, Psyche, when she visits the place of souls, is advised to abstain from food. Kohl found the myth among the Ojibbeways, Mr. Codrington among the Solomon Islanders; it occurs in Samoa, in the Finnish Kalewala (where Wainamoinen, in Pohjola, refrains from touching meat or drink), and the belief has left its mark on the mediæval ballad of Thomas of Ercildoune. When he is in Fairy Land, the Fairy Queen supplies him with the bread and wine of earth, and will not suffer him to touch the fruits which grow "in this countrie." See also "Wandering Willie" in *Redgauntlet*.

Page 152. *The latest minstrel.* "The sound of all others dearest to his ear, the gentle ripple of Tweed over its pebbles, was distinctly audible as we knelt around the bed and his eldest son kissed and closed his eyes."—Lockhart's *Life of Scott*, vii., 394.

Page 161. *Ronsard's Grave.* This version ventures to condense the original which, like most of the works of the Pleiad, is unnecessarily long.

Page 162. *The snow, and wind, and hail.* Ronsard's rendering of the famous passage in Odyssey, vi., about the dwellings of the Olympians. The vision of a Paradise of learned lovers and poets constantly recurs in the poetry of Joachim du Bellay, and of Ronsard.

Page 166. *Romance.* Suggested by a passage in *La Faustin*, by M. E. de Goncourt, a curious moment of poetry in a repulsive piece of *naturalisme*.

Page 171. M. Boulmier, author of *Les Villanelles*, died shortly after this *villanelle* was written; he had not published a larger collection on which he had been at work.

Page <u>177</u>. *Edmund Gorliot.* The bibliophile will not easily procure Gorliot's book, which is not in the catalogues. Throughout *The Last Maying* there is reference to the *Pervigilium Veneris*.

Page <u>207</u>. *Bird-Gods.* Apparently Aristophanes preserved, in a burlesque form, the remnants of a genuine myth. Almost all savage religions have their bird-gods, and it is probable that Aristophanes did not invent, but only used a surviving myth of which there are scarcely any other traces in Greek literature.

Page <u>236</u>. *Spinet.* The accent is on the last foot, even when the word is written *spinnet.* Compare the remarkable Liberty which Pamela took with the 137th Psalm.

> *My Joys and Hopes all overthrown,*
>   *My Heartstrings almost broke,*
> *Unfit my Mind for Melody,*
>   *Much more to bear a Joke.*
> *But yet, if from my Innocence*
> *I, even in Thought, should slide,*
> *Then, let my fingers quite forget*
>   *The sweet Spinnet to guide!*

Pamela, or Virtue Rewarded, vol. i.,
., 1785.

Printed by BALLANTYNE, HANSON & Co.

Edinburgh London

FOOTNOTES.

[35] Cf. "Suggestions for Academic Reorganization."

[46] The last three stanzas are by an eminent Anthropologist.

[48] Thomas of Ercildoune.

[66] A knavish publisher.

> [88] Vous y verrez, belle Julie,
> Que ce chapeau tout maltraité
> Fut, dans un instant de folie,
> Par les Grâces même inventé.
>
> 'À Julie.' *Essais en Prose et en Vers*, par Joseph Lisle; Paris. An. V. de la République.

[108] "I have broken many a pane of glass marked Cruel Parthenissa," says the aunt of Sophia Western in *Tom Jones*.

[194] N.B. There is only one veracious statement in this ballade, which must not be accepted as autobiographical.

[196] These lines do *not* apply to Miss Annie P. (or Daisy) Miller, and her delightful sisters, *Gades aditurae mecum*, in the pocket edition of Mr. James's novels, if ever I go to Gades.

[207] Tonatiu, the Thunder Bird; well known to the Dacotahs and Zulus.

[208a] The Hawk, in the myth of the Galinameros of Central California, lit up the Sun.

[208b] Pundjel, the Eagle Hawk, is the demiurge and "culture-hero" of several Australian tribes.

[208c] The Creation of Man is thus described by the Australians.

[209a] In Andaman, Thlinkeet, Melanesian, and other myths, a Bird is the Prometheus Purphoros; in Normandy this part is played by the Wren.

[209b] Yehl: the Raven God of the Thlinkeets.

[210a] Indra stole Soma as a Hawk and as a Quail. For Odin's feat as a Bird, see *Bragi's Telling* in the Younger Edda.

[210b] Pundjel, the Eagle Hawk, gave Australians their marriage laws.

[210c] *Lubra*, a woman; kobong, "totem;" or, to please Mr. Max Müller, "otem."

[210d] The Crow was the Hawk's rival.

[232] Lycaon, the first werewolf.

www.ingramcontent.com/pod-product-compliance
Ingram Content Group UK Ltd.
Pitfield, Milton Keynes, MK11 3LW, UK
UKHW040820280325
456847UK00003B/569